KIDS ON THE BALL

USING SWISS BALLS IN A COMPLETE FITNESS PROGRAM

Anne Spalding

Linda Kelly

Joanne Posner-Mayer

Janet E. Santopietro

Human Kinetics

Library of Congress Cataloging-in-Publication Data

Kids on the ball : using Swiss balls in a complete fitness program /
by Anne Spalding . . . [et al].
    p.   cm.
    Includes bibliographical references.
    ISBN 0-88011-714-1
    1. Physical fitness for children.   2. Balls (Sporting goods)
3. Movement education.   4. Physical education for handicapped
children.   5. Physical education and training.   I. Spalding, Anne,
1959-   .
GV443.K464   1999
372.86--dc21

98-45908
CIP

ISBN: 0-88011-714-1

Developmental Editor: C.E. Petit, JD; **Assistant Editors:** Cassandra Mitchell and Kim Thoren; **Copyeditor:** Bonnie Pettifor; **Proofreader:** Sue Fetters; **Graphic Designer:** Robert Reuther; **Graphic Artist:** Tara Welsch; **Cover Designer:** Jack Davis; **Photographer:** Gary Hacking/Photography G, **except** page 6 by Mary Spalding and page 134 by Rick Santopietro; **Illustrator:** Mary Yemma Long; **Medical Illustrator:** Beth Young; **Printer:** Versa Press

Human Kinetics books are available at special discounts for bulk purchase. Special editions or book excerpts can also be created to specification. For details, contact the Special Sales Manager at Human Kinetics.

Printed in the United States of America   10 9 8 7 6 5 4 3 2 1

Human Kinetics
Web site: http://www.humankinetics.com/

United States: Human Kinetics, P.O. Box 5076, Champaign, IL 61825-5076
1-800-747-4457
e-mail: humank@hkusa.com

Canada: Human Kinetics, 475 Devonshire Road Unit 100, Windsor, ON N8Y 2L5
1-800-465-7301 (in Canada only)
e-mail: humank@hkcanada.com

Europe: Human Kinetics, P.O. Box IW14, Leeds LS16 6TR, United Kingdom
+44 (0)113-278 1708
e-mail: humank@hkeurope.com

Australia: Human Kinetics, 57A Price Avenue, Lower Mitcham, South Australia 5062
(08) 82771555
e-mail: humank@hkaustralia.com

New Zealand: Human Kinetics, P.O. Box 105-231, Auckland Central
09-523-3462
e-mail: humank@hknewz.com

CONTENTS

PREFACE

It's colorful, big, and enticing. Both children and adults are attracted to the Swiss Ball. No one can resist using it. In recent years, innovative teachers have introduced the Swiss Ball, previously used only for therapy, into educational settings. Now classroom teachers, physical educators, and physical therapists use this unique tool to help children develop balance, coordination, rhythm, and fitness skills.

The authors of this book are three physical educators and a physical therapist. We have used the balls in our programs and have seen the growth in our students. In the process of sharing our ball programs at conventions and workshops, we recognized the need for a comprehensive book about the Swiss Ball. Teachers asked, "We have these balls, but what can we do with them? How can we use them in our existing programs? What objectives do the activities meet? How do the activities fit content standards?" We will answer these questions in this book.

Kids on the Ball is written for all professionals who work with children and are interested in developing optimal balance, coordination, rhythm, and fitness. It will help teachers plan stimulating and exciting lessons using the unique medium of the Swiss Ball. In *Kids on the Ball* we will

- describe activities using the ball,
- discuss modifications for special needs students (mainstreamed or not),
- address safety procedures, management, and care of the ball,
- provide curriculum ideas for incorporating the Swiss Ball into your present program,
- integrate Gardner's Theory of Multiple Intelligences and different learning styles, and
- incorporate content standards and benchmarks (NASPE and APENS).

Part I is about the foundations for using Swiss Balls. Chapter 1 discusses why you should use Swiss Balls. Chapter 2 outlines how to use the Swiss Balls in physical education, classroom, and therapy settings. Chapter 3 explains how to get started: selecting the correct balls, inflating them, and using them safely.

We have organized part II by developmental skills so you can integrate the Swiss Ball activities throughout the school year. Chapter 4 explains how to select activities, the progression within the modules, learning center and whole class formats, and special considerations for inclusion of children with special needs. Chapter 5 describes balance activities. Chapter 6 covers coordination activities. Chapter 7 outlines rhythm and dance activities. Chapter 8 includes flexibility activities. Chapter 9 shares muscular strength and cardiorespiratory fitness activities, including a complete sample workout. Chapter 10 covers manipulative skills activities. And chapter 11 describes games using the Swiss Ball. To make your job easier, this part of the book also includes reproducible charts.

In part III, we use the activities in part II to outline a Swiss Ball curriculum, including assessment techniques and forms. After discussing planning and assessment in chapter 12, chapters 13 through 16 present lesson plans for preschool through sixth grade students. Finally, chapter 17 shares tips for and stories about how to integrate the Swiss Balls into the regular classroom.

We hope sharing our experiences and enthusiasm for the Swiss Ball will motivate you to include this piece of low-impact equipment. It will enrich and enhance your program, providing immeasurable benefits to your students. So let's get on the ball!

Acknowledgments

Over the years, we have participated in a wide range of seminars and conferences at which we met many people and discussed many different activities and uses for Swiss Balls. We would like to express our appreciation to those professionals who helped us by responding to questionnaires, granting interviews, or providing information and guidance on specific topics discussed in this book. We apologize to anyone we have inadvertently left out.

Anna Duval, *Adams County (Colorado) School District*

Carole Huffman, *Aspen Elementary, Aspen, Colorado*

Lindsay Ross, *Body Dynamics, Boulder, Colorado*

Anne Turnacliff, *Fireside Elementary, Louisville, Colorado*

Rebecca Hutchins, *Hutchins Vision Therapy, Boulder, Colorado*

Dominick Maino, *Illinois College of Optometry, Chicago, Illinois*

Julie Coleman, *Mesa View Elementary, Grand Junction, Colorado*

Shirley Stafford, *Montview Preschool, Denver, Colorado*

Sue Berg, Bridget Matthews, Quinn Reed, Kathryn Krauser-Yokooji, and Barb Zoeller, *Riverdale Elementary, Thornton, Colorado*

Ilyne Engle, Nancy Lyneis, Leslie Gertin, Cheryl Moore, Patty Toomey, and Donna Gilbert, *Rocky Mountain Elementary, Westminster, Colorado*

Linda Hanson, *Westley Elementary, Westley, Wisconsin*

PART I

Foundations for Using Swiss Balls

CHAPTER 1

WHY USE SWISS BALLS?

"The best athletics of all are those that not only exercise the body but are able to please the spirit."
—*Galen, Greek physician, 2nd century AD (Sweet, 1987)*

The value of using balls to enhance health has been recognized since the notable Greek physician, Galen. The ball "can stir the enthusiast or the slacker, can exercise the lower portions of the body or the upper, some particular part rather than the whole, or it can exercise all of the parts equally . . . [it] is able to give the most intense workout and the greatest relaxation." (Sweet 1987) The large, colorful Swiss Balls attract children and adults like a magnet. They have been used for over 30 years with people of all ages and abilities to address all four types of exercise: aerobic, stretching, strengthening, and relaxation. In addition, they have been used to improve balance, coordination, postural control, and sensory integration. This chapter offers a therapist's point of view of physical exercise and, especially, spinal health in children and the lifelong benefits of using the Swiss Ball. Use the related activities in chapter 5 to educate your students about the negative effects of a sedentary lifestyle as well as the positive effects of physical activity on the spine.

Statistics from the medical community in industrialized countries show that 80% of the adult population suffers from back pain (Mayer and Gatchel 1988). Next to the common cold, back pain is the main reason for lost days at work, and it also causes people to miss the social and recreational activities they enjoy. To change these statistics, we need to start educating children about back care before they form bad postural habits and problems arise. We have fought the battle of tooth decay with education. It is now time to fight back pain because, unlike your teeth, your spine is irreplaceable.

We have inherited bodies from our prehistoric ancestors that were designed for the strenuous, active life of the hunter gatherer, not our modern sedentary lifestyle. Most back pain results from the years of poor posture, static sitting, improper body mechanics, and general deconditioning prevalent in modern society (Saunders 1995). Every day we make choices that will effect the quality and duration of our lives. Some choices, like smoking, have direct consequences we can detect almost immediately. Others, like poor posture, lack of exercise, inadequate flexibility, and deficient balance have indirect effects and consequences that may take decades to detect.

Poor Posture, Back Pain, and Stiffness: Why?

People are less active. For children, liability issues often keep schools from offering many types of beneficial exercise equipment, such as high slides, merry-go-rounds, etc. This fear of lawsuits has also lead to more supervised activities and fewer activities that encourage independent exploration. At home, many children watch television or play computer games rather than engage in active play and, in many areas, are kept indoors or in small backyards due to the risks of unsupervised play in the neighborhood. Kindergartners still get plenty of activity; however, by fifth grade, children are already showing the postural deconditioning effects of sitting both in school as well as in their free time.

Keeping the spine and all other joints flexible is not only very important for the health of the tissues, but also for having good balance reactions while performing daily activities and sports. Unfortunately, repetitive activity causes some muscle groups to get stronger and shorten, which can stretch out weaker opposing muscles and thus cause joint restrictions. For example, think of students and adults who work at desks. Their back muscles get weakened and stretched out from the slouched posture, but the shoulder muscles in the front of the body tighten (shorten) from all the time they spend seated with their arms in front of them. Then, in order to look forward at a computer or chalkboard, their necks have to compensate into an arched (extended) and forward position. This results in tightened neck muscles and shoulder tension, which can lead to headaches and wear and tear on the neck and shoulder joints. The stretching exercises using the ball in chapter 7 are highly recommended to keep the spine flexible throughout a person's life.

Besides the other benefits of exercise, there is a correlation between physical activity and good postural control. Fifty years ago, very few jobs existed where one could earn a living sitting down all day; however, many adults now work in office jobs which promote inactivity and, depending upon the workstation, poor posture. Poor posture not only causes wear and tear to the spine but it can also significantly decrease lung capacity and impair circulation to nerves, muscles, and the brain. Driving, television, and computers lead to less activity after work. The Swiss Ball can be used as a chair at a desk or computer to promote active sitting and, when muscle tension occurs, it can be used as a tool to stretch over and relax at brief intervals during the work day.

Keeping active and flexible can also help mitigate other problems related to spinal health. One of these stems from the fact that the discs between the vertebrae receive no direct blood supply after age 10 so all nutrition and circulation to the spine depends on physical activity (Olive and Middleditch 1991). Reduced movement hinders circulation to the disc. Eventually, stiffness (in arthritis) from degeneration of the disc or pain can occur from bulging discs pressing on these nerves. This process can take 40 years or can happen quickly due to injury. But once there is pain, it can be very hard to get rid of and for half of the people who have back pain once, it will return later.

When Swiss Balls are used in schools, you are taking the first step toward educating children about the importance of movement, exercise, and spinal health. Good posture does not require a lot of muscle strength. It requires muscle endurance; in other words, the muscles need to do a little bit of work for a long period of time. Beginning with active sitting, in which you replace an ordinary chair with a Swiss Ball, you convert the sedentary act of sitting to a beneficial activity. If a ball is used as a chair, there is no back support to lean against and it is a dynamic, unstable surface. More muscles are activated around the spine for postural support and the feet, legs, and hips have to work to maintain balance. The ball makes it impossible to sit totally still for long periods (Headley 1996), leading to active, dynamic sitting. This allows circulation to the structures of the spine, making sitting more active like standing. Active sitting in a good posture will help prevent wear and tear caused by lack of circulation and uneven pressures on the discs that occur in bad posture.

Active sitting also improves balance because, as a dynamic base, the body "drifts" when it is relaxed. The muscles in the ankles, knees, hips, lower back, and abdomen return the body to center where the body is at its most efficient. These little muscle movements stabilize the spine and improve core control and, consequently, balance. As you study and use this book, keep in mind that good balance skills not only prevent accidental falls, they also improve the ability to perform a variety of sports. *Your body was meant to move—not sit still!*

Using the Swiss Ball also promotes cardiovascular fitness. An exercise routine using the ball is a low-impact alternative to high-impact activities such as running, jumping rope, and traditional aerobics. To demonstrate the difference between high-impact activities and Swiss Ball exercises with students or other interested parties, try some of the cardiovascular exercises described in chapter 9 using the balls. For example, have the children compare the effects of doing 10 jumping jacks while sitting on the ball with doing 5 jumping jacks while standing. Discuss the differences between impact on the joints and amount of physical activity between the two activities.

It is important to remember that your students have probably never thought or been taught about spinal health. At most, they've heard their parents tell them to "sit up straight." You can present spinal health in a positive light with the fun activities that open chapter 5. Then, when you begin to use the Swiss Ball activities, you can explain to the students how the Swiss Ball enhances spinal health and creates good lifetime postural habits.

Educators in Switzerland have found that when children understand and use these concepts themselves, they also teach other people in their family to be aware of good posture (Illi 1994). Children can be very persuasive with their parents concerning matters of health and longevity! The Swiss Ball is a perfect tool for anyone to use to learn or teach these lessons in a fun and rewarding manner.

CHAPTER 2

WHO CAN USE SWISS BALLS?

We want to encourage physical educators to join forces with physical and occupational therapists, sharing expertise and resources to achieve success for all students in all settings. Thus, in this chapter, we will address several collaborative issues: communication among professionals about students who are receiving or who could benefit from receiving services, sharing and adapting exercises and equipment, and designing collaboration programs. Also in this chapter, we'll discuss how to help students with sensory integration dysfunction. Finally, we'll offer sample exercises and activities that are safe and appropriate for students with special needs.

Collaborating Among Specialists

Collaboration among the various specialists working with an individual student with disabilities is vital to meeting the needs of the student. Effective collaboration, however, doesn't simply happen; it is earned through hard work and dedication to serving the best interests of the child. Specifically, three components comprise effective collaboration: communicating effectively, sharing and adapting equipment, and designing formal collaboration programs. To begin collaborating in your situation, tackle each of these areas in the order we present here. Then, work to keep all three areas running smoothly.

Communicating Effectively

As individual needs of students with disabilities become more diverse, physical educators often must help more and more mainstreamed students who are receiving occupational and/or physical therapy. Thus, effective communication among physical educators and physical and occupational therapists is indispensable when working with a diverse population of students. Yet even when occupational and physical therapists work in the same building with physical educators, these three groups rarely find the time to sit down and talk about their students and their programs. Specifically, each of us—no mat-

Swiss Balls help therapists & teachers work together

ter our specialty—must ask ourselves what we can do to increase the comfort of mainstreamed students.

Where should you start? Complete student records can sometimes be difficult to obtain and are not always easy to read and understand. However, physical and occupational therapists are familiar with medical and therapy terms and concepts, and are generally happy to share strategies and techniques that will reinforce their work. Indeed, if you have students with special needs in your physical education classes, the input from therapists can mean the difference between designing lessons that are developmentally appropriate and lessons that are frustrating or dangerous.

Of course, we all want the physical education environment to be safe and productive, but meeting so many diverse needs can be challenging. To add to the complexity, you might observe possible physical delays or disorders other teachers have not seen, because the physical education curriculum and environment is more dynamic than many regular classrooms, thereby highlighting these problems. And, like many physical educators, you may experience some guilt when students leave your gym without having their needs met.

To meet individual needs better, ask questions and seek information from other staff members who work with your students to give you a more complete profile of each student's abilities and disabilities. Of course, you should consult with the special education and the regular classroom teacher. In addition, if a student is receiving support from a private occupational or physical therapist or both, you should contact these professionals as well. Parents are generally happy to provide therapists' phone numbers so instructors can get specific information about a child's therapy after the parents send the appropriate consent form. You'll find that therapists and parents will be pleased when you design lessons that support the efforts of the therapists, appropriately challenging the student in the physical education setting.

Therapists also benefit from the teacher's insights. Therapists can provide extra support when they're aware of the teacher's current and planned lessons. Teachers can also improve therapy by sharing information on a child's progress, problems, and physical interactions with other students that may not be obvious from a therapist's one-on-one sessions.

Sharing and Adapting Exercises and Equipment

Swiss Balls provide a common ground upon which therapists and physical educators can build cohesive programs. Many therapists are either using the balls in their work or are at least familiar with them. Students with cerebral palsy often use the balls to help with stretching and strengthening muscles or normalizing muscle tone. Many students receiving therapy for coordination disorders, lack of balance, or lack of strength often use the Swiss Balls to help alleviate problems. You can find out the specific exercises and the precautions therapists take when working with students with specific disabilities. At the very least, add a mat for extra padding even though other students in your class may not need this precaution.

Slow the pace for these students and otherwise adapt the exercises to meet their specific needs. It is often difficult for these students to perform leg and arm movements at the same time, so help them discover the part of the exercise they feel most comfortable with. Then instruct students to keep their feet flat on the floor and move only their arms or to grasp the ball with their hands and attempt the leg and foot movements only. Be sure to demonstrate the exercises in their modified forms. Meanwhile, give students who face an extra challenge as much encouragement as they need to keep them on task, making your comments as specific as possible.

Because physical therapists and physical educators who collaborate all want to use the same equipment with certain students, sharing equipment is an economical way to meet these students' needs. You may even be able to combine funds and purchase items such as physio-rolls, Swiss Balls, mats for cushioning, resistive bands, and other manipulative tools. Although sharing equipment entails a little extra planning, it may be the only way to meet the needs of a diverse population on a tight budget. As a bonus, exchanging equipment naturally leads to an opportunity for sharing expertise and knowledge of students' needs. Indeed, we have found the working relationships we developed through sharing equipment were possibly more valuable and beneficial to the students than the equipment itself!

Designing Collaboration Programs

Opening up the lines of communication and sharing equipment are preliminary steps toward true professional collaboration. However, although scheduling problems and time restraints may seem daunting, it is possible for teachers and therapists to work more closely together—the rewards far exceed the effort.

Formal Visits

By inviting therapists into your gymnasium to observe the progress of students who are receiving special services, you will give them the opportunity to make more accurate assessments of students in a dynamic, whole-class setting. Conversely, when you as a physical educator visit therapy sessions, you can learn more about how to help a student.

Visits from and to therapists can also be of great value if you are uncertain as to how best to ease the transition for newly mainstreamed students. As part of the transition process, encouraging therapists to conduct their sessions in the gymnasium during regular class time alleviates the isolation some special needs students feel. They are able to participate alongside other students while receiving the extra support, guidance, and expertise they require. This approach also allows students who do not receive services to get to know a therapist, who may have been a stranger in the hall up until this time.

Therapists can also learn a great deal during classroom visits. Observing students in the classroom environment—with its noise, clutter, and constant interactions—will demonstrate how well a given student has integrated therapy results into daily living. The therapist can also adapt his or her program to the skills and sports she observes the other children trying to master, which will aid inclusion of disabled students in the regular program.

Motor Labs

Another way of uniting forces is to conduct a "motor lab." This is a specific time before, after, or during the school day when specialists team up to help any students in the school who would benefit from extra help in the motor areas. These labs require a commitment from all the specialists involved, because it will take time to plan, organize, and implement this type of program. To get started, first identify students who could use the help. This may include students who are well behind their peers in motor skill proficiency, but who are not considered disabled. Next, send permission slips home to obtain parental consent. Finally, plan and organize activities to meet each student's needs. While students may be hesitant to participate in the labs at first, they will quickly come to see the experience as a highly desirable "double PE" class.

You probably won't have trouble choosing activities, but keep groups small to ensure plenty of individualized assistance for students. We have conducted motor labs with as many as 30 students working with three specialists and three or four parent volunteers; these labs worked because the parents were very reliable and competent. Ideally, you should have a ratio of four or five students to one adult.

Learning centers are our favorite way of organizing a motor lab group. To use learning centers effectively, begin by instructing the whole group, then break up into specific work areas. It is helpful to create a variety of centers and to have enough centers to keep groups small. You may want to include a center that coincides with your current physical education theme or focus skill. Therapists may prefer to work on different skills and with different equipment, and the learning center format provides enough flexibility for a wide variety of activities. A successful motor lab may combine, for example, learning centers using long and short jump ropes, scooter boards with incline ramps, barrels and wedges for rolling, and Swiss Balls and physio-rolls. Students love a variety of stimulations! Best of all, the extra time and expertise you have all shared with the students gives them more confidence in performing skills.

Addressing Sensory Integration Dysfunction

You need a basic knowledge of therapeutic techniques and specific tools to effectively integrate students with sensory integrative disorders in more productive, yet fun, learning experiences. But first, what is *sensory integration*?

Defining Sensory Integration

Sensory integration (SI) keeps our daily lives running smoothly not only when we are awake but also while we are sleeping. It is the interconnection of all of the senses that allows us to move through space confidently, coordinating what we see, hear, and feel in our environment (Ayres 1979).

The incidence of sensory integrative problems has increased due to the higher survival rate of premature infants born with immature nervous systems. In fact, SI problems are now common among children worldwide. Unless the dysfunction is severe, these problems may be overlooked by anyone who is not trained to recognize them. Most physical educators, however, have taught children with sensory motor difficulties, such as those with attention deficit disorder, hyperactivity, or mild autism. These children stand out because of one or more of these characteristics: noticeable clumsiness, fidgety behaviors, lack of attention and self-discipline, or difficulties with peer interactions and following directions. Dealing with these children can be challenging and often frustrating because regular discipline methods don't seem to be effective in controlling these behaviors. And often, unfortunately, these difficulties disturb the entire class.

Sensory integration disorder was first recognized and identified by Dr. Jean Ayres, an occupational therapist, over 30 years ago. Her definition of sensory integration is the "neurological process that organizes sensation from one's body and from the environment and makes it possible to use the body effectively within the environment." She further defines sensory integration as the ability of the central nervous system to organize and process input from different channels to make an adaptive response (Ayres 1979). As you know, all the information we receive about the world comes to us through the sensory system.

When dealing with our daily routines, we are simultaneously bombarded with a variety of sensations (stimulation). Some are distinct, such as touch, sight, sound, and smell. Others are less obvious, such as the force of gravity and body position in space. Some sensations catch our attention more than others. Some we respond to, and others we disregard. The ability to filter the information and focus on that which is meaningful depends on an efficient sensory integrative system. People who can interpret the sensory information from their surroundings adequately are able to respond successfully, meeting the challenges of the environment. An effective response, in turn, may lead to orientation and learning.

For example, imagine yourself at a party on a boat where many conversations are taking place around you. At the same time, someone is talking to you, one on one. To understand what the speaker is saying, you need to be able to disregard other conversations, focusing on what is meaningful to you. If at the same time you smell smoke, you need to be able to decide if it is harmless or dangerous, while still paying attention to the person talking to you. Meanwhile, the music is getting louder, and it becomes harder to hear the person talking to you. To complicate matters further, the boat starts to sway side to side, and you struggle to keep your balance while still listening to the person talking to you. To meet this myriad of sensory challenges, you must rely on successful past experiences, which allow you to automatically make proper adjustments by moving closer to the person talking, spreading your feet apart, and holding onto something stable to keep your balance—all while looking in the direction of the smoke. Successfully combining these responses depends on a working sensory integrative system that creates a new adaptive response specific to the demands of this unique environment. Most likely, you take this all for granted as you successfully manage the situation.

People with sensory integration disorders find even common sensations and situations confusing, frightening, or overwhelming. For school children, the commotion of the classroom, playground, and gym may be enough to disorganize their sensory processing systems. But how, do you identify children who may require expert testing to diagnose sensory integrative problems?

Signs of Sensory Integrative Dysfunction

The signs of a child or adult with sensory integrative dysfunction will often include being either underreactive or overly sensitive to touch, movement, sight, or sound. The overly sensitive individual may withdraw from touch, avoid certain textures of food or clothes, and be fearful of common movement activities found on a playground. They may also be easily irritated and distracted. Another characteristic might include an unusually high activity level, constantly on the move (hyperactive) or an unusually low activity level, slow to become active and fatiguing easily (hypoactive).

Coordination, motor planning and execution, and balance might also be impaired, making the individual appear clumsy as he often trips, falls, or bumps into things. Not surprisingly, this child avoids participating in movement activities and games. Moreover, he often avoids even simple tasks, such as reaching across the midline of the body, alternating feet on stairs, or using two hands at the same time. Indeed, activities of daily living—automatic for most of us, such as going through a doorway—may be a challenge.

Difficulties with speech, language, motor skills, or academic achievement may remain unrecognized during the preschool years despite normal intelligence. Poor organization of behavior, such as inability to pay attention, inability to properly sequence a task, or inappropriate excessive movements, may reveal itself through difficulty adjusting to new situations. Children may display impulsive, distractible, aggressive behaviors or become frustrated and withdraw when they encounter failure. Usually, these problems lead to poor self-concept, resulting in problems with peer interaction and academics.

Intervention With Swiss Balls

A therapist certified in SI treatment will use many pieces of specialized equipment in her clinic to help the child achieve the proper sensory motor integration. Ramps, scooter boards, modified swings, and nets for climbing are common tools. The therapist often expands the treatment to school and home settings, but to achieve the same level of treatment, adjusts the equipment. To this end, the Swiss Ball can be an integral tool in meeting the needs of a child with sensory integrative deficits in a variety of settings.

The Alert Program

Like all good teaching, a good SI program has a plan. *Sensory diet* is a term used to describe a series of strategies designed to help children with sensory integrative problems. The sensory diet, consisting of carefully planned natural activities and sensory inputs, is usually incorporated in what is called the Alert Program. This involves using facilitation techniques to help children monitor, maintain, or change how alert they feel (Williams and Stellenburger 1996). This program helps the child adapt to different situations and tasks. Moreover, the cognitive domain comes into play as the child becomes involved and active in modulating her own level of arousal.

The Alert Program is usually designed by a trained therapist then implemented by the educator, family, or child himself.

Swiss Ball Strategies for Sensory Integrative Deficits

Dr. Jean Ayres has created specific treatment strategies to integrate and improve sensory motor processing skills (Ayres 1972); these form the core of the following Swiss Ball strategies, each of which can either arouse or calm. Use them to create a sensory diet that will meet each special student's needs.

- Rocking or bouncing on a Swiss Ball can either calm or arouse an individual, depending on his need.
- Combine bouncing on a Swiss Ball with sounding out words, spelling, learning math, or memorizing facts. The bouncing should match the rhythm of the task. Rhythm and rhyme facilitates memory while bouncing enhances the respiratory patterns.
- Combine the following activities with sitting on a Swiss Ball to promote better control of posture and alertness.
    - Oral motor play with a texturized object such as a flexible rubber tubing, a cloth, or teething toys (under the supervision of a therapist) promotes the ability to focus and proper organization of behavior. Chewing and biting also improves the the dynamic control of the jaw, neck, shoulder, and pelvis (Oetter 1993).
    - Using natural fragrances stimulates the olfactory system and higher levels of the central nervous system (limbic system) to increase or decrease arousal level and trigger memory and emotions.
    - Implement a brushing program with children having difficulty processing tactile information. The brushing program uses a surgical brush to firmly brush the skin of the back, arms, and legs with back and forth strokes (Wilbarger 1991). Activities using the ball, especially bouncing and rolling, allow the child to be actively involved in treating sensory defensiveness through active deep touch.
    - Wearing a weighted vest, using weighted balls, or resistive pushing and pulling stimulate the proprioceptive system. This system tells the brain about the body's position and movement in space. Proper

stimulation of this system promotes stability, ability to grade (properly adjust) movement forces, and internal organization.

- Sucking activities promote visual focus and enable the production of speech sounds made at the back of the mouth (k, g,). Blowing promotes visual focus and eye tracking for far vision as well as the sounds that require graded air flow (f, s, sh, chz, n, h) (Oetter 1993).

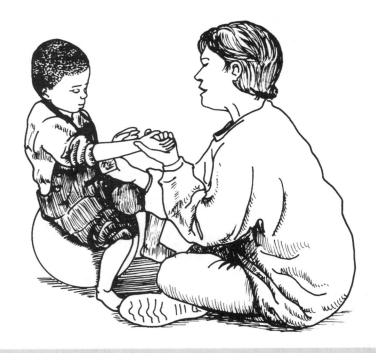

An example of brushing.

Use the following information to see how sensory integration works and practical ways to use the Swiss Balls in school settings—the regular or special education classroom and the physical education program. Help identify children struggling with sensory integrative disorders, and in collaboration with a trained motor therapist, employ exercises to help these students succeed or at least have a positive experience.

Enhancing Sensory Integrative Skills in Physical Education

Everyone associates a ball with fun and games. When the students see the balls in the gym, the colors and the desire to touch and explore the movements the balls offer will stimulate their interest. Indeed, the ball or physio-roll will motivate children with special needs to participate in physical activities when they might otherwise feel discouraged and hesitant because they lack coordination and fear movement (postural insecurity). Note, however, to mainstream physically challenged students safely, you may need to use a mat underneath the ball or physio-roll.

The therapeutic benefits Swiss Balls offer to enhance sensory integration skills are numerous:

Aerobic exercises improve cardiovascular and respiratory functions and therefore improve arousal.

The freedom to run (or simulate the building blocks of running while sitting and bouncing on a ball) and experience different speeds of movement allows for developing body and spatial awareness besides grading of movement.

The openness of the space allows for experimenting with timing for rolling, dribbling, or bouncing and catching the balls, which also addresses bilateral integration (coordination of the two sides of the body).

Imitating someone else's movements and verbal instructions requires the processing of visual and auditory information. The large ball is unstable and dynamic, which forces many systems of the body to work together to control movement, besides stimulating alertness and attention to task. It makes these activities more fun and it is challenging to manipulate.

Stretching exercises also require active participation for balance and promotes vestibular stimulation (by changing the head position in space), influencing the arousal state (see chapter 8).

Peer interactions and self-esteem can be enhanced by doing group exercises including special needs children (who may need assistance) with children without disabilities.

The opportunity to exercise in pairs enhances cooperative play. At the same time you can explore body and spatial awareness, tactile input, and motor planning skills.

Using music or rhymes stimulates memory, sequencing skills, and rhythmic beat competency.

Holding hands while sitting or lying on a ball provides tactile input and social skills requiring cooperative interaction for team building.

Enhancing Sensory Integrative Skills in the Classroom

So far we have primarily addressed ways in which the physical educator can extend a student's physical or occupational therapy program in the gym. In this section, we'll show you how a regular classroom or special education teacher can use the Swiss Balls in the classroom.

Introducing the ball into the classroom as a therapeutic tool primarily for "active sitting" is valuable in itself. The children's behavior will be proof of improved sensory organization. The ball can become an even more powerful tool when combined with guidance from a trained therapist who can help you meet the individual requirements of a special needs child. So consult with a trained therapist when designing and evaluating such a program.

Specifically, replacing the standard stable classroom chair with an unstable ball that moves can be therapeutic because it does the following:

Activates postural muscle control, resulting in better hand control

Improves visual skills for improved focusing, tracking, and scanning

Stimulates the vestibular sense for better balance reactions and alertness

Stimulates proprioception for better muscle control and force of movement

> Coordinates the two sides of the body for improved midline orientation
>
> Improves pronunciation of words by promoting jaw stability through improved postural control

Each of these benefits enhances sensory processing, thereby increasing alertness and sustained attention, which, of course, facilitates learning.

If the ball has not been previously introduced to the students by the physical educator, the classroom teacher might either plan an exploratory session of free play or introduce the ball in a more structured situation such as just sitting on it at table activities or story time. This depends on the teacher's judgment of the classroom needs. (See chapter 3 for safety guidelines.) Children with attention deficit disorders usually respond well with this approach.

Start with two or three balls in the classroom, letting the children take turns. If the special needs child does better on the ball, allow him to have it for longer periods and slowly add more balls as the other children adapt to them. Once the students are familiar with the ball, they can begin to use it in various other structured ways in the classroom setting. Therapeutic experiences may include sitting on the ball for tabletop activities, such as art activities (drawing, cutting, painting), writing, reading, snack time, and using manipulatives (puzzles, blocks, beads). Sitting on the ball when working at an easel or wall may improve grasp, visual skills, and upper body strength (Williams and Shellenburger 1996). Students may sit or lie over the ball for group time activities, such as story time and music time, movement exercise, and oral motor group exercises to improve control of muscles of the neck, shoulder, jaw, tongue, and face, and lip control for better production of language, sounds, and eating skills.

Under supervision of a trained therapist, the classroom teacher can create a sensory diet, including rocking on the ball in various positions; bouncing while sitting, which changes level of alertness; and combining the ball with other SI techniques, such as brushing, chewing, and weights with proper positioning on the ball. These activities should remain under a therapist's one-on-one supervision, even after creating teacher awareness of their value.

Summary

Using sensory integration techniques with the ball in the classroom and gym not only helps students with SI dysfunction improve their self-organization levels and regulate their behavior, but also ensures pleasant learning experiences for the other students as well as teachers. To develop a safe and effective treatment plan that meets the individual needs of each child with sensory integration dysfunction or any other disability, be sure to consult with either a physical, occupational, or speech therapist trained in treating the particular problem. Joining forces with other specialists is an educational experience for all concerned. Everyone will learn new ways to help children with special needs.

CHAPTER 3

HOW DO I GET STARTED?

A Swiss Ball therapy program must be safe and effective. To provide a safe environment, become acquainted with ball sizing, instructions for inflating the balls, safety tips and considerations, and correct use of the balls. This chapter should prevent or resolve any confusion or complications that may arise while using the Swiss Balls.

The Ball Is the Thing

Choosing the right tool for the job works with Swiss Balls as in other areas. Use these tips to select, inflate, fit, and use the Swiss Balls correctly.

Selecting the Correct Ball Size

Fit a Swiss Ball according to a person's body proportions. Make sure that hips and knees are positioned at a 90-degree angle when seated on the ball (Klein-Vogelbach 1990, Kucera 1974). If a person's height is between two specifications, she has long legs, or she is overweight, you may need to use a larger ball. When in doubt, we recommend a larger ball, because you can adjust it by slightly underinflating it to accommodate an individual (see table 3.1). The most commonly used ball sizes for elementary and middle school students range from 45 centimeters to 55 centimeters in diameter; however, taller and heavier students and average and larger teachers need a 65-centimeter ball.

Fitting the Ball to the Individual

Most students and adults will be drawn to the largest ball available. You will have to educate participants as to how to select a safe and effective ball. You must help them understand that a properly inflated and a correctly sized ball maximizes both safety and physical benefit.

TABLE 3.1 — RECOMMENDED BALL SELECTION

PERSON'S HEIGHT	BALL SIZE
Children 1-2 yrs	30cm — 12 inches
Children 3-5 yrs	35cm — 14 inches
5 yrs to 4'11"	45cm — 18 inches
5' to 5'7"	55cm — 21 ½ inches
5'8" to 6'2"	65cm — 25 inches
6'3" to 6'9"	75cm — 29 ½ inches
Over 6'10"	85cm — 33 ½ inches

Adapted from Posner-Mayer (1995).

Figure 3.1   Front view

To accommodate students of different sizes and abilities, vary ball sizes from underinflated to the maximum recommended diameter. Heavy students and those who are physically and/or mentally challenged will achieve the greatest success with a larger, underinflated ball. Students in this category may include REACH students (students who are two standard deviations below the average IQ and are learning life skills); students with physical limitations resulting from organic conditions, such as cerebral palsy or muscular dystrophy; and emotionally and behaviorally disturbed students. In addition, the physio-roll, a ball shaped like a peanut, offers an excellent alternative to the round Swiss Ball for many students in this category.

Sitting Correctly on the Swiss Ball

You cannot be sure a ball fits unless an individual is sitting on it correctly. Figures 3.1 and 3.2 demonstrate how to sit on a Swiss Ball correctly. Notice that a 90-degree angle provides the optimal leg position for good posture while sitting. To provide maximum stability and correct posture, have participants position their feet hip-width apart and point their toes forward. A ball that is too large will increase the angle at the knees and hips, causing an individual to slouch backward. Be sure you help each individual select the correct size ball—a ball that is too small decreases the angle at the knees and hip, causing knee and hip discom-

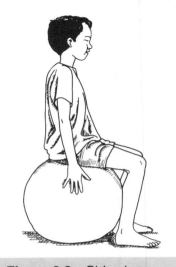

Figure 3.2   Side view

fort. Model how to select the ball, then place several copies of the figures around the room (enlarged if necessary) so students can use it to select a ball that fits properly. You can also have students use the figures to assess each other's ball selection.

Inflation Instructions

When you unpack a new Swiss Ball from the box, examine the contents. You should have a ball and a plug or stopper. If the box is crushed during shipment, a slight possibility exists that the ball has been damaged. So, before inflating a ball, check for any damage and notify the supplier if your ball is damaged or if you have questions. Then, before each use, inspect for gouges, deep scratches, and punctures. Do not attempt to repair a ball if it has been punctured or gouged. Note, too, that a plug puller is available to remove valves for easy deflation.

The balls will not properly inflate unless they are at room temperature. Moreover, the balls require a high volume of air at low pressure, so a bicycle pump, which produces a low volume of air at high pressure, will not work well. Electric air compressors and manual air raft or mattress pumps that have a cone-shaped nozzle are best. Car or tire repair facilities usually have an air compressor, which you can use to fill up a few balls at a time. Ask for a cone-shaped (trigger) nozzle.

You must inflate the balls according to size, not pressure (figure 3.3). Most balls have the maximum diameter printed on them. Overinflating a ball will stretch the vinyl too thin, reducing its strength. As mentioned, a ball may be used slightly underinflated, but, remember, it should be large enough so the user's hips and knees are bent at 90-degree angles when sitting on it.

To monitor inflation, use a yardstick or tape measure to mark maximum diameter (height) for the ball on a wall or door. Then pump air into the ball. Put

Figure 3.3   Pre-marking ball size on the wall makes measuring easy.

the plug in the ball and measure the ball by placing a yardstick on top of the ball and comparing it with the mark on the wall or door. Add or release air as necessary. Do not inflate the ball larger than the maximum diameter specified.

Safety First

You must take two key safety precautions, one regarding floor space and the other regarding students' work space. Follow these guidelines each class period to ensure your students' safety.

Safety Instructions

You can take several simple classroom environment precautions to make Swiss Ball use safer. First, since a ball can be damaged by rolling over a sharp object, check the floor *each class period* for sharp objects, such as rocks, pins, thumbtacks, and staples. Sweep the floor with a vacuum, broom, or mop to be sure. Check student clothing and jewelry to ensure it cannot damage the balls as well. Second, define each student's work space. We recommend skid-proof rubber spots, carpet squares, or some other visual aid to help students stay in self-space while working with the ball. The natural inclination is to move closer to your partner or group. Since it is essential to have space between participants, provide enough unobstructed space so no furniture or other objects in the immediate area can cause injury. In addition, keep the ball away from direct sunlight or other sources of heat for extended periods of time.

Maintain optimal posture when bouncing. Do *not* combine bouncing with bending, twisting, or rotating the spine.

Dress for Success

Participants should wear comfortable clothes that allow full range of movement. Denim jeans or other tight-fitting pants are usually too restrictive for ball exercises. Shorts should be at least knee length as bare skin will often stick to the ball, hindering movement, and, possibly, causing discomfort.

When participants come to class wearing athletic shoes they have worn outside, have them check the soles for pebbles. These may fall out of the soles and puncture the ball if it happens to roll over them. In addition, we recommend rubber-soled shoes. Finally, a heavy pony tail may cause discomfort to the neck and so may need to be modified.

Introducing the Swiss Ball

Emphasize safety precautions when introducing students to the balls. Be sure, for example, to discuss back and head injuries *before* you bring out the balls. Teach them to understand and take responsibility for their own bodies.

Follow these steps, which integrate science with physical education, to teach Swiss Ball safety. Adjust the depth of detail to the students' age and ability.

1. Ask students to raise their hands if they know someone who has had a back or head injury.

2. Next display a picture, poster, or model of the skeletal system. Reproduce and use figure 3.4 at this time.

3. Have students name and point to any bones they know.

4. Explain how the brain, spinal cord, and body are connected.

5. Have students touch their heads while you explain that under the hair and scalp and inside the skull is the brain, which is approximately the size of both of their fists put together.

6. Show students a poster of the internal organs and point out the brain and the spinal cord.

7. Explain that the brain is the command center for all bodily functions and that messages travel up and down the spinal cord, connecting the brain with the rest of the body. It is helpful to illustrate the concept by giving some examples: when we want to run, jump, or climb stairs, the brain sends the message down the spinal cord to the nerves in our legs; when we reach for something that is hot and may burn us, the nerves in the hand send a message up the spinal cord to the brain, and the brain sends an immediate message back down the spinal cord and out to the nerves in the hand, telling the hand to pull away.

8. Finally, tell students that the vertebrae are the bony structures which protect our spinal cord. Explain that if we are hit or fall very hard, the vertebrae may not be strong enough to protect the spinal cord. Make it clear to them that when the spinal cord is damaged it can no longer transmit messages to and from the brain. Gently reassure students that knowing how their bodies work will help them to prevent injuries. Emphasize the fact that we would never want to do anything on the ball that might cause us to injure our vertebrae or spinal cord or cause us to hit our head.

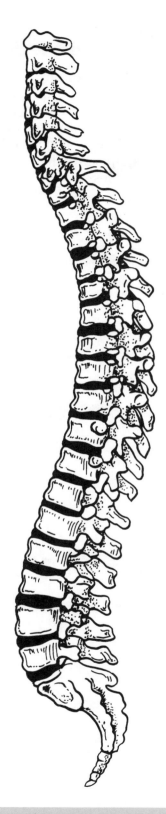

Figure 3.4　Adult spine

Summary

As in any area of physical activity, you must put safety first when using the Swiss Balls. Follow the guidelines in this chapter for selecting, fitting, inflating, and using the Swiss Balls to prevent injury and facilitate learning (see also appendix A for maintenance). Use the lesson provided to discuss Swiss Ball safety before bringing out this exciting tool. With proper care and precautions, your equipment will last and your students will enjoy safe and productive Swiss Ball lessons for many years to come.

PART II

Activities With Swiss Balls

CHAPTER 4

SELECTING ACTIVITIES

Now that you know how valuable the Swiss Ball can be and how to use it safely, let's turn to creating a developmentally appropriate program that is right for you, your students, and your teaching situation. In this chapter, we'll show you how to select activities based on the National Association for Sport and Physical Education (NASPE) Standards and benchmarks. Then we'll suggest a progression of activities for all ages and ways to organize the learning environment. Finally, we'll address the inclusion of special needs students, including discussing the Adaptive Physical Education National Standards (APENS).

To get started on the selection process, first review your yearly plan, highlighting the benchmarks you are focusing on for each grade level. Next glance through chapters 5 through 11 to see which standards and benchmarks the Swiss Balls meet. You will find the Swiss Balls will fit into a large number of content areas.

You will be able to use the Swiss Balls in two ways: to introduce skill themes, such as balance, and to integrate, reinforce, enrich, and enhance activities in your P.E. curriculum, such as fitness and manipulative use, throughout the school year. In introductory activities, we find the Swiss Balls generate tremendous enthusiasm for the skill themes we are working on. In three or four lessons (50 minutes each), you can introduce a variety of activities for students to practice (see chapters 13 through 16). Next, as you revisit these skill themes in depth during the year, you can integrate Swiss Ball activities into the practice of those skills.

The NASPE Standards and benchmarks found in *Moving Into the Future* (1995) were written in an open-ended fashion to allow you to incorporate specialized activities such as the Swiss Balls. We have included both the NASPE and the Swiss Ball benchmarks throughout the book to help guide you.

The progression of beginning activities we recommend is as follows:

- Sitting on the Ball Correctly (Activity 5.7)
- Hip Movements (5.8)
- Balancing with arm moves (5.9)
- Basic Bounce (6.1)
- Check Stop (6.2)
- Bouncing with arm moves (6.3 through 6.12)

- Balancing with foot moves (5.10 through 5.14)
- Bouncing with foot moves (6.13 and 6.14)

Note that bouncing activities are interspersed with balance activities because no one can sit still on the ball. So don't bother to attempt to stifle this natural impulse to bounce. Just be sure to teach the Check Stop immediately after the Basic Bounce. The best plan is to alternate between dynamic and static activities, such as in the following example:

- Prone Balance (Activity 5.17)
- Prone Balance with arm and leg lifts (5.17)
- Side Balance (5.24)
- Side Stretch (8.2)
- Tabletop Balance (5.22)

After you have taught this basic progression and provided ample practice time and safety training, feel free to use any of the activities and skill themes found in:

- Chapter 7—Rhythm and Dance,
- Chapter 8—Flexibility,
- Chapter 9—Muscular Strength and Cardiorespiratory Fitness,
- Chapter 10—Manipulative and Gymnastic Skills, and
- Chapter 11—Games.

To make planning even easier, we have organized each of the skill theme chapters from simple to complex skills.

Organization

There are two basic approaches you can take to organizing the Swiss Ball learning environment: learning centers and whole class instruction. In this section, we'll discuss the logistics of how to organize your students and equipment for either situation. In addition, we'll outline in detail how to safely and efficiently distribute and collect the balls for each situation, sharing with you the methods we have found to be most successful. We encourage you to apply the following management suggestions to create safe, productive lessons.

Learning Centers

As mentioned in chapter 2, we recommend introducing students to the balls through a learning center format. In this section, we'll look closely at how to organize and teach through learning centers.

Learning Center Organization

If, for example, you set up several learning centers based on activities you have already taught your students and one center using the balls, most of your students can practice independently while you concentrate on the group you are introducing to the balls. We have found that this varies depending on your equipment and students' ability to work independently in learning centers. Students who are working in learning centers without you must be self-motivated and able to work independently on the chosen task. Each group should include no more than six students.

This organizational method will keep the entire class on task while you focus on teaching specific new skills on the Swiss Ball. Choose a theme (e.g., fitness) and plan several centers in separate areas, such as jump ropes, simple obstacles courses, strength exercises (e.g., wall push-ups or crunches), and your Swiss Ball center. As your students become familiar with the balls, you can increase the number of learning centers devoted to Swiss Ball activities as equipment allows.

First introduce and discuss the Swiss Ball center to the whole class, referring to the lesson in safety as described in chapter 3. Then divide students into evenly sized groups. The size of your learning centers will vary depending on the specific activities, the number of students participating, and the number of centers. It is wise to handpick students for groups with the knowledge you have of their specific social and physical abilities. As with other activities, when using the Swiss Balls, it is fine to combine a variety of skill levels in one group because they can be role models for one another. Like most teachers, you are probably always striving for positive social interaction, and you know best how to mix your students for a positive experience.

Learning Center Strategies

The following are specific suggestions for organizing a safe and effective learning center lesson:

- Create a "ball pen" of sorts by placing the balls behind cones, a bench, on deck tennis rings, or in inverted steps, in each designated learning center to keep balls still and evenly spaced. The balls need to be stored in the learning center so that each group comes and takes a ball that fits correctly without the balls rolling. Students need space to pick up a ball and quickly and safely move to a spot on the floor where there is a marker. Place floor markers of some type (e.g., poly-spots, carpet squares) inside each designated area to show students specifically how much room they will need to safely carry out the prescribed exercises.
- When groups come to the Swiss Ball learning center, have them sit on the floor markers for instructions and a safety review.
- Next have students take the balls from their resting places and place them on the floor markers to begin working.
- Orient yourself so you can keep an eye on everyone in all the learning centers.
- Double-check to ensure your other learning centers are safe, review-oriented centers that do not require much—if any—direct instruction. If not, quickly modify as needed.
- It is possible to move from several learning centers to two centers by splitting the class in half if you have enough equipment. In this case, have

half the students using one side of the gym do, for example, shuttle runs with partners or small groups while the other half works on stretching and strength exercises on the balls.

- Mount posters of the specific Swiss Ball exercises students are practicing on the gym walls at the ball learning centers.

Whole Class Participation

Once your students are more familiar with using the balls, you may wish to have everyone use them simultaneously. Be especially attentive to safety, however, as 20 bouncing students may seem more like 40! Indeed, emphasize the need to maintain self-space to prevent collisions.

One of our favorite techniques for whole class instruction uses overhead illustrations. We play soft music while overhead transparencies are placed on a projector. This strategy allows the teacher to walk around the room and assist students with postural and mechanical adjustments. The close proximity of the teacher moving through the students helps limit the noise level and any potential behavior problems. Having the students concentrate to replicate the illustration on the screen keeps them focused.

Whole Class Organization

As you may imagine, good organization is essential when having your entire class use the Swiss Balls at the same time. Separate the balls into four storage areas, such as the four corners of your gym. Make ball pens as for learning centers by blocking the balls in with whatever you have that will hold them in place. Scatter floor markers near these storage areas to designate self-spaces, clearly defining safe work areas for students to begin trying out moves once they have chosen their balls.

Choosing the Balls

Follow this procedure for choosing balls:

1. Have students walk to the nearest storage area and take turns picking out a ball, then walk to their self-spaces and begin.
2. Encourage students to take a good look at the posters illustrating the correct sitting posture when they choose a ball.
3. Have them check with a friend to be sure the ball is the proper size.

Whole Class Strategies

If you employ a variety of teaching strategies simultaneously, each student will achieve success quickly and pleasurably. For students who prefer direct and visual input, put up posters to illustrate different exercises and balancing moves. You can accommodate curious students who are simply aching to interact and be creative with the balls by setting aside a safe exploration area for them. This is a time to watch students carefully for safety and for great new ideas you can use later. You can even allow students to demonstrate these creative new movements—a good way to start any ball lesson.

Putting the Balls Away

Instruct students to return the balls to the nearest corner of the room. Use the following suggestions to maintain safe and appropriate behavior:

- Tell students to walk, not run, and to take turns placing the balls where they were originally stored.
- Create a parade, such as in the game "Follow the Leader." Be sure to emphasize control and safety at this time.
- Demonstrate placing the ball gently on the ground in a storage area.
- Do not allow students to throw, bounce, or kick the balls to a storage area.

Special Needs Students

As discussed in chapter 2, it is easy to include special needs students in Swiss Ball lessons. To this end, all the lessons in chapters 5 to 11 include helpful adaptations. In addition to using physio-rolls or underinflated balls and padded surfaces as mentioned in chapter 2, have a paraeducator help each special needs student sit up straight and balance on the ball, according to the disability, by stabilizing the student at the hips.

In addition, we have listed the Adaptive Physical Education National Standards (APENS) with each activity. Use them to guide you as you strive to meet the needs of students with disabilities.

These APENS Standards apply throughout the book:

10.01 Teaching Styles: Demonstrate Various Teaching Styles in Order to Promote Learning in Physical Education

- Provide clear, concise, and simple language when needed.
- Use specific, clear, concise verbal cues to highlight points.
- Perform demonstrations with verbal cues to maximize sensory information input.
- Establish a physical activity environment that remains the same in terms of format, procedures, and routines for individuals with disabilities such as autism, mental retardation, and blindness.
- Guide students to be peer tutors or partners to teach individuals with disabilities.
- Design activities that allow individuals to work together in pairs.
- Design activities and instructions to the ability level of the individual with disabilities, such as using picture activity cards to depict the desired skill to be performed.
- Design for a variety and modification of equipment in each activity to ensure successful completion of each assigned task.
- Select tasks that can be performed by the individual with a disability individually and safely.
- Identify and create goal levels for each skill or activity that will allow all individuals with disabilities to achieve levels of success at the same task.
- Design the class activities in a circuit type or station arrangement (learning centers).
- Use individualized charts and reports to determine the progress of individuals with disabilities.

- Use praise and feedback to foster alternative methods of completing the skill or task.
- Use group activities to promote cooperative learning development.
- Use group activities to foster incidental learning, such as social values and interaction skills in individuals with disabilities.

10.02 Teaching Behaviors: Understand the Various Teaching Behaviors Needed to Promote Learning

- Assess skill development and progress using a skill- or student-specific task analysis testing tool (qualitative) that also accounts for level of independence and dependence during evaluation and teaching.
- Teach the correct form necessary to perform the skill.
- Establish lesson activity sequence that alternates high and low intensity activities to foster fitness improvement.
- Play cooperative games that foster social interactions and trust for individuals with and without disabilities.
- Design activities for individuals with disabilities that provide knowledge of performance through auditory and visual feedback.

10.04 Preventive Strategies: Understand Preventive Management Strategies in Order to Promote Learning

- Use paraprofessionals and peer tutors for individuals who require greater attention.

Summary

You can present and use the Swiss Balls in learning center or whole class format. We recommend introducing the Swiss Balls in one learning center while the rest of the class reviews previously learned skills using other equipment. However, unify the lesson by choosing a single theme for all your centers. Try a whole class format once your students are familiar with the Swiss Balls and have demonstrated they can use this equipment safely. Finally, refer often to the Adaptations and APENS sections to help special needs students get the most out of each activity.

CHAPTER 5

INTRODUCTION TO SPINAL HEALTH AND BALANCE

The Swiss Ball offers an opportunity for students to test and practice balancing on a safe, nonthreatening piece of equipment. The activities are unlimited and offer students the opportunity to explore and practice movements that are appropriate and challenging for their own developmental stages. But first in this chapter, we'll share activities to help make students aware of the need for spinal health. Then, we'll describe the balance activities we have used successfully.

Introduction to Spinal Health

Educators in Switzerland have concluded that children can be very persuasive when it comes to matters of health care. Specifically, they have discovered that children who understand and apply spinal health and physical activity concepts to their own lives persuade others in their families to be aware of good posture and how it affects them. So use the following activities to begin to turn each student into a spinal health advocate.

WHAT'S IMPACT?

Purpose

To show how the world interacts with and creates forces (gravity, compression, inertia) affecting the body.

Aspect

Cognitive.

NASPE Standards (1995)

Standard 2, benchmark for kindergarten: Identifies and begins to use the technique employed, such as leg flexion to soften the landing when jumping.

Procedure

Direct students to do the following:

1. Walk around the activity area for 30 to 60 seconds.
2. Run around the activity area for 30 to 60 seconds.
3. Jump up and down four times.
4. Compare how the impact of each activity affected the joints as their feet hit the ground.

Questions

- Raise your hand if you've ever heard someone say, "Oh, my back hurts!"
- Raise your hand if you would like to share your own personal experience with back pain. (This may lead to stories about parents and grandparents with back pain, bringing the message closer to home.)

Key Point

- To avoid back problems, learn about your spine and form good lifetime habits to take care of it, like you do with your teeth.

GETTING THE MOST OUT OF A DEEP BREATH

Purpose

To compare and contrast the difference between taking a deep breath while slouching and sitting correctly.

Aspect

Cognitive.

NASPE Standards (1995)

Standard 4, benchmark for kindergarten: Understands the importance of breathing during movement.

Procedure

Direct students to do the following:

1. Sit up straight and take in a deep breath, then raise both hands as high over the head as possible. Exhale and return to normal position.
2. Slouch over and attempt a deep breath, then attempt to raise both hands over the head.
3. Compare the difference in air intake in both positions.

Questions

- How might breathing while slouching affect sport performance?
- How might breathing while slouching affect performance in everyday life?

Key Points

- More air fills your lungs when you're sitting or standing up straight.
- Less air fills your lungs when you're slouching.
- More air means more oxygen.
- Your body functions more efficiently and effectively when it has more oxygen.

MOVING TOWARD A HEALTHIER SPINE

Purpose

To illustrate you can avoid wear and tear on the spine by standing and sitting correctly and by moving around slightly while you are sitting for long periods, as you do while standing.

Aspect

Cognitive.

NASPE Standards (1995)

Standard 1, benchmark for kindergarten: Understands that correct alignment is beneficial to health.

Procedure

After arranging students in a circle around you, direct them to do the following:

1. Freeze in whatever position they assumed.
2. Discuss, "Who is slouching, and who is sitting up straight?"
3. Sit up straight and tall.
4. Discuss, "Do you have to work hard to sit up straight?"
5. Sit straight for one minute, without moving.
6. Discuss, "How hard is it to stay sitting up straight for a minute? Predict how hard it would be to stay in that position for five minutes."
7. Stand up.
8. Repeat steps 1 through 6.

Key Points

- When standing, the spine moves because you unconsciously sway slightly to keep balanced.
- When sitting, you are more conscious of your movements to avoid slouching.

BE A SLINKY

Purpose

To test range of motion and teach that stretching increases flexibility (see also chapter 8).

Aspect

Cognitive.

NASPE Standards (1995)

Standard 1, benchmark for kindergarten: Understands concept of flexibility.

Procedure

Direct students to do the following:

1. Bend over forward and arch backward while standing.
2. Bend sideways and return to center. Repeat on the other side.
3. Look over one shoulder, twisting around to see as far behind yourself as is comfortable.
4. Repeat the motion looking over the other shoulder.

Key Points

Use a slinky to demonstrate these points:

- Keeping the spine and all other joints flexible is important to maintain healthy tissue. (Pull slinky straight up.)
- A combination of flexibility and good balance makes movement easier, making daily activities and sports easier. (Pull and bend slinky to one side and then the other side.)
- When adults or children stop moving through the full range of motion, they eventually become stiffer, because muscles and ligaments tighten up if their motion isn't used. (Compress the slinky to its smallest shape.)

PREVENTING SWAYBACKED POSTURE

Purpose

To emphasize the importance of routinely stretching hip and upper leg muscles to prevent stiffness of the back.

Aspect

Cognitive.

NASPE Standards (1995)

Standard 2, benchmark for kindergarten: Understands concept of stretching and stiffness.

Procedure

Direct students to do the following:

1. Stand up and lean their trunks forward while bending slightly only at the hips.

2. Mimic swaybacked posture by freezing the flexed hip position (achieved in step 1) and straightening the spine to look straight ahead.

3. Walk around the room in the posture described in step 2.

4. Try running a few steps in swaybacked posture. How does it feel?

Key Points

- Walking and running in a swaybacked position are uncomfortable.

- Swaybacked positions do not look or feel good.

PROPER LIFTING AND BENDING

Purpose

To prevent back injury and pain by bending and lifting properly.

Procedure

Direct students to do the following:

1. Place your feet in a wide stance with one foot forward and close to the object you're lifting and the other foot close to where you're placing the object.

2. As you lift the object, bring it in close to the body.

3. Swivel your feet to face the other direction, keeping your spine straight instead of lifting and twisting your spine.

4. Practice this sequence using the Swiss Ball or an imaginary object.

5. Compare bending over while keeping your knees and legs straight to bending your knees and lifting with your legs.

Key Points

- Back injuries are caused by bending and lifting objects using improper body mechanics.
- Keep the spine straight as you lean forward. Bend down using your hips and knees so you're using the large strong muscles of your legs and buttocks to do the lifting instead of the small, weak muscles of your spine.
- To avoid painful back injuries, don't twist while lifting.

Balance Activities

What exactly is *balance*? Balance is the ability to maintain a body position against the force of gravity and keep the center of gravity over the base of support. Balance may be either static or dynamic. A static balance is fixed, or in a stationary position, while dynamic balance is maintained while the body is moving. Balance (also called *stability skills*) is a fundamental movement skill upon which all other movement depends. Indeed, balance is basic to all we do.

Using three different sensory systems develops balance: visual (ocular), auditory (vestibular), and tactile (kinesthetic and proprioceptive). Thus, activities emphasizing these three systems help improve balance. Integrating these three systems facilitates optimal balance. An individual develops good balance through doing activities against gravity that mobilize the automatic balancing reaction and improve spinal stability. An individual can improve his overall ability to balance by balancing on the ball in three different positions: sitting, prone, and supine.

Balancing While Sitting on the Ball

Activities sitting on the ball develop core control (trunk control) and upright balance (postural control). The following are specific activities that improve these skills.

5.7

SITTING CORRECTLY ON THE BALL

Purpose

To improve spinal stability by sitting correctly on the ball.

Aspect

Balance.

NASPE Standards (1995)

Standard 1, benchmark for kindergarten: Maintains momentary stillness bearing weight on a variety of body parts.

Prerequisite Skills

Ability to balance on the ball while sitting.

Procedure

Direct students to do the following:

1. Sit in the center of the ball with feet in front on the floor.
2. Make feet and knees face forward.
3. Keep knees and feet hip-width apart.
4. Sit up as straight as possible—tall, chin in, shoulders back.
5. Maintain 90-degree angle of knees.

Key Points

- Lightly touch hands to ball to help balance.
- Keep spine aligned in optimal posture (see chapter 1).

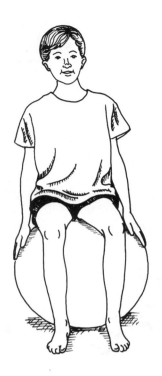 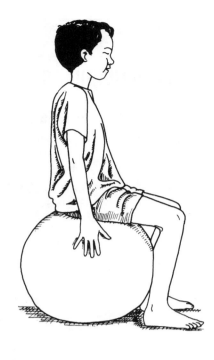 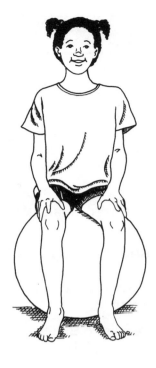

Variations

- Relax arms at sides without touching ball.
- Place hands on thighs.

Adaptations

- Use physio-roll or underinflated ball.
- Have a paraeducator assist student, according to disability.

APENS (1995)

Standard 2.01: Implement activities that stimulate upright postures and control of head, neck, and trunk.

Standard 6.06: Adapt equipment.

Standard 10.04: Use paraprofessionals and peer tutors for individuals who require greater attention.

HIP MOVEMENTS

Purpose

To improve spinal mobility and to test the automatic balancing reaction with hip movements while seated on the ball.

Aspect

Maintaining balance during dynamic hip movements.

NASPE Standards (1995)

Standard 1, benchmark for kindergarten: Maintains momentary stillness bearing weight on a variety of body parts.

Prerequisite Skills

Ability to sit correctly on the ball.

Procedure

Direct students to do the following:

1. Side to Side: Using hips, gently roll ball from side to side as far as possible, allowing ankles and knees to move.

2. Forward and Backward: Roll ball forward and backward as far as possible, using hips and allowing knees and ankles to move. Keep feet planted and allow lower spine to curve and arch.

3. Circle Hips: Move ball in a circle, using hips (as if spinning a hula hoop) and allowing knees and ankles to move. Move hips clockwise and counterclockwise.

Key Points

- Keep feet hip-width apart and firmly planted for proper body alignment.
- Keep shoulders level.
- Start with small movements.
- For safety's sake, move smoothly, slowly, and with control.
- Touch ball with hands to help balance.

Variation

- Gradually make movements larger.

Adaptations

- Use physio-roll or underinflated ball.
- Have paraeducator assist student, according to disability.

APENS (1995)

Standard 2.01: Implement activities that stimulate upright postures and control of head, neck, and trunk.

Standard 6.06: Provide activities that increase pressure on body surfaces, joints, and muscles, such as pushing and pulling.

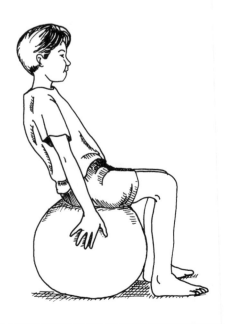

BASIC ARM MOVEMENTS

Purpose

To test spinal mobility and the automatic balancing reaction with seated arm movements.

Aspect

Balance.

NASPE Standards (1995)

Standard 1, benchmark for second grade: Balances, demonstrating momentary stillness, in symmetrical and asymmetrical shapes on a variety of body parts.

Prerequisite Skills

Ability to sit correctly on the ball.

Procedure

Direct students to do the following:

1. Sit on the ball correctly.
2. Raise both arms to sides of body until even with shoulders.
3. Hold, lower arms, and repeat.

Key Points

-   Sit on the ball correctly.
-   Keep shoulders level.
-   Raise arms smoothly, slowly, and with control.

Variations

-   Arms Overhead: Raise both arms to sides of body until hands are directly overhead.
-   Asymmetrical Arms: Touch hands to shoulders with elbows out to sides. Lift elbows to shoulder height. Reach one arm up and one arm out. Return hands to shoulders and alternate sides.

Adaptations

-   Use physio-roll or underinflated ball.
-   Have paraeducator assist student, according to disability.

APENS (1995)

Standard 2.01: Implement activities that stimulate upright postures and control of head, neck, and trunk.

Standard 6.06: Adapt equipment.

HEEL LIFT

Purpose

To test spinal mobility and the automatic balancing reaction with heel movements while seated on the ball.

Aspect

Balance.

NASPE Standards (1995)

Standard 1, benchmark for second grade: Balances, demonstrating momentary stillness, in symmetrical and asymmetrical shapes on a variety of body parts.

Prerequisite Skills

Ability to sit correctly on the ball.

Procedure

Direct students to do the following:

1. Sit on the ball correctly.
2. Raise both heels off floor while toes remain in contact with floor, hold, then lower.
3. Repeat.

Key Points

- Keep shoulders level.
- Raise heels smoothly, slowly, and with control.
- Touch hands to ball to help balance.

Variations

- Heels Apart and Together: Lift right heel and pivot on ball of foot so heel swings away from center. Return heel to start. Repeat with left foot. Next, alternate right and left heels. Finally, move both heels at same time.
- Heels Side to Side: Lift both heels from floor, pivot on balls of feet, and swing heels left, then right. Knees should be together and swinging in opposite directions from heels.

Adaptations

- Stabilize student at hips.
- Use physio-roll or underinflated ball.
- Have paraeducator assist student, according to disability.

APENS (1995)

Standard 6.06: Use simple to complex skills.

Standard 6.06: Use gradual balance progression from static to dynamic.

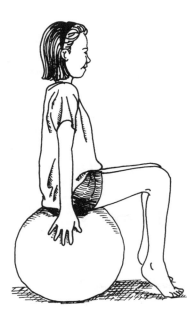
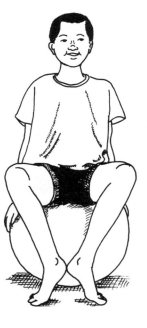

TOE LIFT

Purpose

To test spinal mobility and the automatic balancing reaction with toe movements while seated on the ball.

Aspect

Balance.

NASPE Standards (1995)

Standard 1, benchmark for second grade: Balances, demonstrating momentary stillness, in symmetrical and asymmetrical shapes on a variety of body parts.

Prerequisite Skills

Ability to sit correctly on the ball.

Procedure

Direct students to do the following:

1. Sit on the ball correctly.
2. Raise both toes off floor, keeping heels on floor, hold, then lower.
3. Repeat.

Key Points

- Sit on the ball correctly.
- Keep shoulders level.
- Raise toes smoothly, slowly, and with control.
- Touch ball with hands to help balance.

Variations

- Toes Apart and Together: Lift right toe and pivot on heel of foot so toe swings away from center. Return toe to start. Repeat with left foot. Next, alternate right and left toes. Finally, move both toes at same time.

Adaptations

- Stabilize student at hips.
- Use physio-roll or underinflated ball.
- Have paraeducator assist student, according to disability.

APENS (1995)

Standard 2.01: Develop and implement programs that stimulate vestibular, visual, and proprioceptive senses.

Standard 6.06: Use gradual balance progression from static to dynamic.

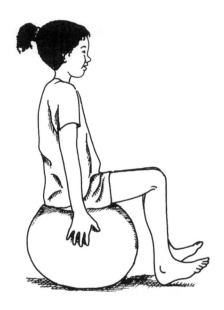

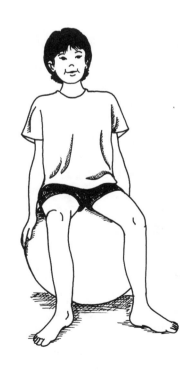

SIDE TOE TOUCH

Purpose

To test spinal mobility and the automatic balancing reaction with foot movements while seated on the ball.

Aspect

Balance.

NASPE Standards (1995)

Standard 1, benchmark for second grade: Balances, demonstrating momentary stillness, in symmetrical and asymmetrical shapes on a variety of body parts.

Prerequisite Skills

Ability to sit correctly on the ball.

Procedure

Direct students to do the following:

1. Sit on the ball correctly.
2. Lift right foot off floor and touch toe to right side, extending leg. Hold and return to center.
3. Repeat with left foot.
4. Continue to alternate.

Key Points

- Sit on the ball correctly.
- Keep shoulders level.
- Move smoothly, slowly, and with control.

Variations

- Front Heel Touch: Lift right foot from floor and touch heel forward, extending leg. Hold and return to center. Repeat with left foot. Next alternate right and left foot.
- Sideways Heel Touch
- Front Toe Touch

Adaptations

- With young children, touch foot (instead of toe or heel) to front.
- Stabilize student at hips.
- Use physio-roll or underinflated ball.
- Have paraeducator assist student, according to disability.

APENS (1995)

Standard 2.01: Develop and implement programs that stimulate vestibular, visual, and proprioceptive senses. Structure tasks and activities to stimulate and facilitate normal postural responses.

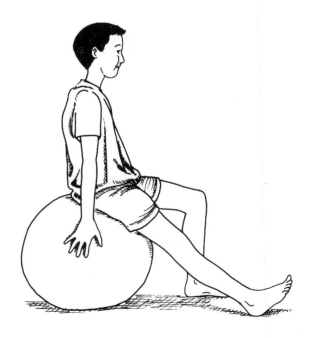

KNEE RAISE

Purpose

To improve spinal stability and test the automatic balance reaction with leg movements.

Aspect

Balance.

NASPE Standards (1995)

Standard 1, benchmark for second grade: Balances, demonstrating momentary stillness, in symmetrical and asymmetrical shapes on a variety of body parts.

Prerequisite Skills

Ability to sit correctly on the ball.

Procedure

Direct students to do the following:

1. Sit on the ball correctly.
2. Lift right knee toward chest, bringing right foot from floor.
3. Hold, then return right foot to floor.
4. Repeat with left foot.
5. Continue to alternate.

Key Points

- Sit on the ball correctly.
- Keep shoulders level.
- Move smoothly, slowly, and with control.
- Lightly touch hands to ball or position arms out to sides to help balance.

Variations

- Leg Lift: Lift right foot off floor and straighten leg. Bend right knee and replace right foot on floor. Repeat with left leg. Continue to alternate.

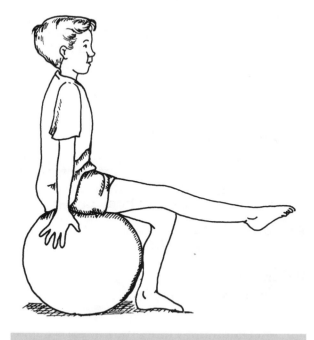

Leg Lift

- Leg Cross and Uncross: Lift right foot and cross over left leg. Replace right foot on floor. Repeat with left foot. Continue to alternate.

Adaptations

- Use physio-roll or underinflated ball.
- Have paraeducator assist student, according to disability.

APENS (1995)

Standard 2.01: Develop and implement programs that stimulate vestibular, visual, and proprioceptive senses. Structure tasks and activities to stimulate and facilitate normal postural responses.

SIDE STRADDLE

Purpose

To test the automatic balance reaction and improve spinal stability with foot jumps while seated on the ball.

Aspect

Balance.

NASPE Standards (1995)

Standard 1, benchmark for second grade: Balances, demonstrating momentary stillness, in symmetrical and asymmetrical shapes on a variety of body parts.

Prerequisite Skills

Ability to sit correctly on the ball.

Procedure

Direct students to do the following:

1. Sit on the ball correctly.
2. Lift knees and feet apart, "jumping" the feet, then bring knees and feet back together to beginning position.
3. Continue to alternate.

Key Points

- Sit on the ball correctly.
- Keep shoulders level.
- Move legs smoothly, slowly, and with control.
- Lightly touch hands to ball to help balance.

Variations

- Forward and Back Straddle: Jump feet so one moves back and the other forward, then switch. Continue to alternate.
- Skier: Jump feet to right, about six inches from the center of the ball. Then jump them to left, about six inches from the center of the ball. Continue to alternate.

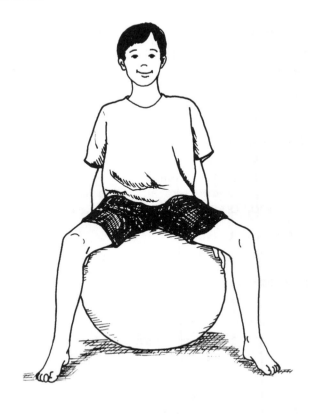

- Bell: Jump feet forward about six inches from front of the ball. Jump feet back to beginning position in front of the ball. Continue to alternate.

Adaptations

- Stabilize student at hips.
- Use physio-roll or underinflated ball.
- Have paraeducator assist student, according to disability.

APENS (1995)

Standard 2.01: Develop and implement programs that stimulate vestibular, visual, and proprioceptive senses. Structure tasks and activities to stimulate and facilitate normal postural responses.

UNILATERAL ARMS AND LEGS

Purpose

To test the automatic balance reaction and increase spinal strength and stability with arm and leg combinations while seated on the ball.

Aspect

Balance.

NASPE Standards (1995)

Standard 1, benchmark for second grade: Balances, demonstrating momentary stillness, in symmetrical and asymmetrical shapes on a variety of body parts.

Prerequisite Skills

Ability to sit correctly on the ball.

Procedure

Direct students to do the following:

1. Sit on the ball correctly with hands on thighs.
2. Extend right leg forward and slightly to side while also lifting right arm up and slightly to side.
3. Return to starting position.
4. Extend left leg forward and slightly to side while also lifting left arm up and slightly to side.
5. Return to starting position.
6. Continue to alternate.

Key Points

- Sit on the ball correctly.
- Keep shoulders level.
- Move smoothly, slowly, and with control.
- Lightly touch opposite hand to ball to help balance.

Variations

- Oppositional Arms and Legs: Swing one arm forward and lift opposite knee. Return to starting position. Repeat on other side. Continue to alternate.
- Alternate Toe Touches With Diagonal Arms: Begin with hands on thighs. Open arms diagonally while touching

Alternate Toe Touches With Diagonal Arms

one foot forward on the toes or ball of the foot. Return arms and foot to start. Repeat arms while touching other foot forward. Continue to alternate.

Adaptations

- Stabilize student at hips.
- Use physio-roll or underinflated ball.

- Have paraeducator assist student, according to disability.

APENS (1995)

Standard 2.01: Develop and implement programs that stimulate vestibular, visual, and proprioceptive senses. Structure tasks and activities to stimulate and facilitate normal postural responses.

5.16

SEATED ROCKER

Purpose

To test the automatic balance reaction and increase spinal strength and stability with whole body movements while seated on the ball.

Aspect

Balance.

NASPE Standards (1995)

Standard 1, benchmark for second grade: Balances, demonstrating momentary stillness, in symmetrical and asymmetrical shapes on a variety of body parts.

Prerequisite Skills

Ability to sit correctly on the ball.

Procedure

Direct students to do the following:

1. Sit on the ball correctly with hands on thighs.
2. Raise arms overhead in a forward direction.
3. Keeping upper body aligned, let the ball roll forward, and lean backward while raising the heels.
4. Hold for a count of five.
5. Rock forward while lowering arms and rolling feet from toes to heels, allowing the ball to roll backward.
6. Hold for a count of five.
7. Repeat.

Key Points

- Sit on the ball correctly.
- Let the ball roll forward and backward.

- Move smoothly, slowly, and with control.
- Avoid arching back. Instead, move from hips.

Adaptations

- Stabilize student at hips.
- Use physio-roll or underinflated ball.
- Have paraeducator assist student, according to disability.

APENS (1995)

Standard 2.01: Develop and implement programs that stimulate vestibular, visual, and proprioceptive senses. Structure tasks and activities to stimulate and facilitate normal postural responses.

Balancing While Lying Prone on the Ball

Activities while lying prone on the ball develop the automatic balance reaction and increase spinal strength and stability.

5.17

PRONE BALANCE

Purpose

To improve the automatic balance reaction and strengthen spinal muscles with prone balances on the ball.

Aspect

Balance.

NASPE Standards (1995)

Standard 1, benchmark for second grade: Balances, demonstrating momentary stillness, in symmetrical and asymmetrical shapes on a variety of body parts.

Procedure

Direct students to do the following:

1. Kneel behind the ball.
2. Place stomach on the ball and put hands on floor in front of the ball.
3. Lift one arm and replace on floor. Repeat with other arm.
4. Lift one leg and replace on floor. Repeat with other leg.
5. Lift two arms and replace on floor.
6. Roll slightly forward, taking weight on hands, lift both legs, then replace on floor.
7. Lift one arm and opposite leg, then replace on floor.
8. Lift both arms and one leg, then replace on floor. Lift both legs and one arm, then replace on floor.
9. Rest chin on the ball.

Key Points

- Stay in self-space.
- Move smoothly, slowly, and with control.
- Take weight on hands or feet or both hands and feet as necessary.
- Gradually increase duration of hold.

Variation

- Lift both arms and both legs.

Adaptations

- Use physio-roll or underinflated ball.
- Pad activity surface.
- Have paraeducator assist student, according to disability.

APENS (1995)

Standard 2.01: Develop and implement programs that stimulate vestibular, visual, and proprioceptive senses. Structure tasks and activities to stimulate and facilitate normal postural responses.

PRONE ROCKING

Purpose

To improve the automatic balance reaction and strengthen spinal muscles with prone rocking on the ball.

Aspect

Dynamic rocking movements.

NASPE Standards (1995)

Standard 1, benchmark for kindergarten: Moves in forward and sideways directions, using nonlocomotor patterns.

Standard 2, benchmark for kindergarten: Identifies and begins to use the technique employed (body flexion) to fall softly and safely.

Prerequisite Skills

Ability to balance in prone position.

Procedure

Direct students to do the following:

1. Kneel behind the ball.
2. Place stomach on the ball and put hands on floor in front of the ball.
3. To create a front-to-back rocking motion, push with both hands to transfer body weight to feet. Then push with feet to transfer body weight to hands.
4. Continue rocking front to back, bending arms and legs to absorb force.

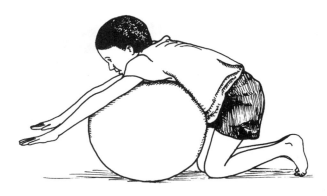

Key Points

- Stay in self-space.
- Move smoothly, slowly, and with control.
- Bend at joints to absorb force of weight transfer.

Variations

- Side to Side: Kneel behind the ball. Place stomach on the ball and spread hands and feet out on floor in front of the ball. To create a side-to-side rocking motion, push against floor with hand and foot on same side to transfer weight to opposite side of body. Then, take weight on hand and foot of opposite side of body. Then push sideways to transfer body weight to opposite side. Continue rocking side to side, bending arms and legs to absorb force.
- Falling: This is an extension of rocking side to side. Roll slowly off one side of the ball with collapsed body parts, transferring weight to side, then the back, and "melt" into floor. Repeat on other side.
- Rolling: On tumbling mats, continue rolling until coming back up on top of the ball. Repeat in opposite direction. Try several in sequence.

Adaptations

- Use physio-roll or underinflated ball.
- Pad activity surface.
- Have paraeducator assist student, according to disability.

APENS (1995)

Standard 2.01: Develop and implement programs that stimulate vestibular, visual, and proprioceptive senses.

Standard 6.06: Use floor spots for "home base."

ASSISTED PUSH-UP

Purpose

To improve the automatic balance reaction and strengthen spinal muscles with an assisted push-up while resting the stomach on the ball.

Aspect

Balance.

NASPE Standards (1995)

Standard 1, benchmark for second grade: Balances, demonstrating momentary stillness, in symmetrical and asymmetrical shapes on a variety of body parts.

Prerequisite Skills

Ability to balance in prone position.

Procedure

Direct students to do the following:

1. Kneel behind the ball.
2. Place stomach on the ball and put hands on the ball under shoulders.
3. Slowly straighten arms, raising chest off the ball.
4. Hold for a count of five.
5. Return to start.
6. Repeat.

Key Points

- Ensure hips remain on the ball.
- Avoid overarching back.
- Keep elbows bent.

Variations

- Extended Prone Push-Up: Pushing with toes, extend legs until body is straight or slightly arched in the back. Then slowly straighten arms, raising chest. Hold for a count of five. Repeat.
- Airplane: From the Extended Prone Push-Up, raise arms out to side. Keep ribs on the ball. Hold for a count of five, then return to start. Repeat.
- Superman and Superwoman: Same as Airplane except extend both arms forward.

Adaptations

- Do the Airplane and Superman and Superwoman from the Prone Push-Up position (on knees).
- Use physio-roll or underinflated ball.
- Pad activity surface.
- Have paraeducator assist student, according to disability.

APENS (1995)

Standard 6.06: Provide activities that increase pressure on body surfaces, joints, and muscles, such as pushing and pulling. Use floor spots for "home base."

Airplane

PRONE WALK-OUT

Purpose

To test the automatic balancing reaction and increase strength of back muscles.

Aspect

Balance.

NASPE Standards (1995)

Standard 1, benchmark for second grade: Balances, demonstrating momentary stillness, in symmetrical and asymmetrical shapes on a variety of body parts.

Prerequisite Skills

Ability to balance in prone position.

Procedure

Direct students to do the following:

1. Kneel behind the ball.
2. Place stomach on the ball with hands and knees on floor.
3. Walk hands out from the ball, letting the ball roll down body toward feet.
4. Walk out as far as strength and balance allow.
5. Walk hands back so stomach is on the ball again.

Key Points

- Stay in self-space.
- Move smoothly, slowly, and with control.
- Keep legs together on top of the ball.
- Keep back straight by tightening abdominal muscles and buttocks.

Variation

- Total Body Flexion: From the Prone Walk-Out, stop when knees are on top of the ball. Pull knees to chest by rolling the ball forward and sit on feet with shins resting on the ball. Relax body in full flexion; then straighten knees and hips to return to start.

Adaptations

- Use physio-roll or underinflated ball.
- Pad activity surface.
- Have paraeducator assist student, according to disability.

APENS (1995)

Standard 2.01: Develop and implement programs that stimulate vestibular, visual, and proprioceptive senses.

Standard 6.06: Use gradual balance progression from static to dynamic.

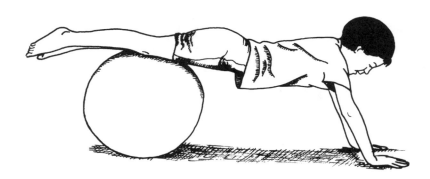

Total Body Flexion

Balancing While Lying Supine on the Ball

Activities while lying supine on the ball develop the automatic balancing reaction and increase the strength of the spinal muscles.

5.21

TABLETOP BALANCE

Purpose

To develop the automatic balance reaction and increase spinal muscle strength with supine balances while on the ball.

Aspect

Balance.

NASPE Standards (1995)

Standard 1, benchmark for second grade: Balances, demonstrating momentary stillness, in symmetrical and asymmetrical shapes on a variety of body parts.

Prerequisite Skills

Ability to sit correctly on the ball.

Procedure

Direct students to do the following:

1. Sit on the ball correctly.
2. Walk feet forward and lean backward while the ball rolls along spine until upper back and shoulders rest on the ball.
3. Hold for a count of five.
4. Walk back up on the ball or gently lower hips to floor.

Key Points

- Move smoothly, slowly, and with control.
- Gradually increase duration of hold.

Variations

- Tell young children that "we are going to make a table," or "we are going to lie down on the ball on our backs." Walk feet forward while rolling ball to under midback. As a challenge, ask them to walk the feet forward a little more (so the ball rolls up their spine even more) and to lift the belly button toward ceiling.
- Advanced Tabletop: Hold Tabletop as described. Lift one foot and straighten knee. Hold for a count of five. Lower foot to floor. Repeat with other foot.
- Add other hand positions as balance improves (e.g., Superman or Superwoman, Airplane).

Adaptations

- Use physio-roll or underinflated ball.
- Have paraeducator assist student, according to disability.
- Pad activity surface.

APENS (1995)

Standard 6.06: Teach wide base of support and low center of gravity.

Standard 2.01: Develop and implement programs that stimulate vestibular, visual, and proprioceptive senses.

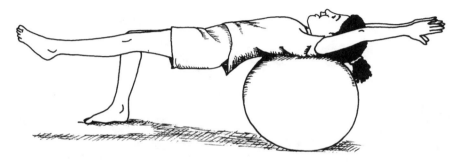

Advanced Tabletop

BRIDGING

Purpose

To improve the automatic balancing reaction and spinal muscle strength with supine balances on the ball.

Aspect

Balance.

NASPE Standards (1995)

Standard 1, benchmark for second grade: Balances, demonstrating momentary stillness, in symmetrical and asymmetrical shapes on a variety of body parts.

Procedure

Direct students to do the following:

1. Lie on back on floor, placing legs on the ball and arms at sides for support.
2. Straighten legs and raise buttocks off floor to form a straight line from shoulders to feet.
3. Hold, then slowly lower body to floor, one vertebra at a time.

Key Points

- Keep spine in optimal posture. Avoid hyperextension.
- Move smoothly, slowly, and with control.
- Gradually increase duration of hold.

Variations

- Place ball farther down legs.
- Pick one leg up off the ball, then write the alphabet with that foot.
- Bridging With Bent Elbows: Lie on back and place legs on the ball, arms at side. Bend elbows, pointing fingers to ceiling.
- Bridging With Raised Arms: Lie on back, place legs on ball, and lift arms off floor, parallel to body.

Adaptations

- Place ball closer to buttocks.
- Only move through partial range.
- Use physio-roll or underinflated ball.
- Have paraeducator assist student, according to disability.

APENS (1995)

Standard 6.06: Teach wide base of support and low center of gravity.

Standard 2.01: Develop and implement programs that stimulate vestibular, visual, and proprioceptive senses.

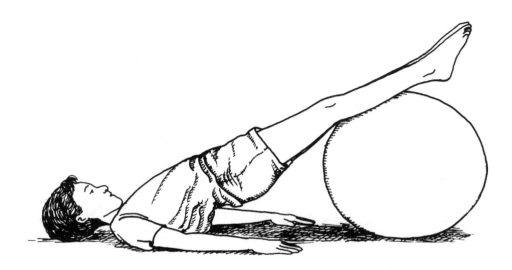

5.23

SIDE BALANCE

Purpose

To improve the automatic balance reaction and strengthen spinal muscles.

Aspect

Balance.

NASPE Standards (1995)

Standard 1, benchmark for second grade: Balances, demonstrating momentary stillness, in symmetrical and asymmetrical shapes on a variety of body parts.

Procedure

Direct students to do the following:

1. Kneel with one side touching the ball and straighten the outside leg away from the ball.
2. Roll the ball and push with both legs while leaning over the ball sideways.
3. Stretch top arm overhead.
4. Hold for a count of five, then gently roll down to starting position.
5. Repeat on other side.

Key Points

- Move smoothly, slowly, and with control.
- Gradually increase duration of hold.

Adaptations

- Use physio-roll or underinflated ball.
- Have paraeducator assist student, according to disability.

APENS (1995)

Standard 6.06: Teach wide base of support and low center of gravity. Provide activities that increase pressure on body surfaces, joints, and muscles such as pushing and pulling.

HAND AND KNEE BALANCE

Purpose

To improve the automatic balance reaction and strengthen spinal muscles through hand and knee balances while on the ball.

Aspect

Balance.

NASPE Standards (1995)

Standard 1, benchmark for second grade: Balances, demonstrating momentary stillness, in symmetrical and asymmetrical shapes on a variety of body parts.

Prerequisite Skills

Abiltity to perform Prone Push-Up.

Procedure

Direct students to do the following:

1. Stand behind the ball.
2. Place hands on the ball shoulder-width apart.
3. Place knees against ball and push forward gently with toes until feet leave floor.
4. Hold for a count of five.
5. Rock back and lower feet to floor.

Key Points

- Transfer weight slowly.
- Push gently.
- Be sure to place hands shoulder-width apart on the ball.
- Place knees hip-width apart on the ball.
- Gradually increase duration of hold.

Variations

- Knee Stand: Move hands near knees, transferring weight to knees. Raise upper body until almost vertical.

Adaptations

- Use physio-roll or underinflated ball.
- Have paraeducator assist student, according to disability.

APENS (1995)

Standard 6.06: Provide activities that increase pressure on body surfaces, joints and muscles such as pushing and pulling. Use simple to complex skills.

CHAPTER 6

COORDINATION

Activities on the ball provide opportunities to achieve motor proficiency, or what we commonly call *coordination*. The Swiss Ball helps children develop efficient patterns of skilled motor behavior while they are having a ball! In this chapter, we'll share activities we have used to develop coordination.

But first, what exactly is coordination? Coordination is the ability to integrate the action of the muscles into efficient movement. Someone who is coordinated can accomplish a specific movement, a series of skilled movements, or complex movements easily and efficiently. In other words, coordination is the harmonious interaction of timing and rhythm in the sequencing of movement. We can also say that the *quality* of an individual's movement performance depends on coordination.

We have arranged the coordination activities in this chapter in a sequential progression. The initial activity is simply whole body bouncing. Then, we explore activities performed by the hands and arms alone—used symmetrically, alternately, and separately—while bouncing. Next, we share activities involving the feet—used separately, alternately, and together—while bouncing. Finally, we progress to combining trunk, hand, and foot movements. Now, let's get started with the Basic Bounce for developing coordination.

6.1

BASIC BOUNCE

Purpose
To develop coordination and posture control.

Aspects
Coordination, balance, and cardiovascular fitness.

NASPE Standards (1995)
Standard 4, benchmark for kindergarten: Supports, lifts, and controls body weight on the ball.

Prerequisite Skills
Ability to sit correctly on the ball with balance.

Procedure
Direct students to do the following:

1. Sit on the ball correctly with hands lightly touching it.
2. Begin bouncing by pushing feet into floor and slightly raising hips and trunk.
3. Relax downward.

Key Points
- Maintain optimal posture.
- Keep feet on floor.
- Begin with small bounces.
- Do not bend or twist spine while bouncing.

Variations
- Ball Taps: Lightly tap the ball while bouncing.
- Thigh Pats: Place hands on thighs. Pat thighs on the downward thrust.

Adaptations
- Have paraeducator assist student, according to disability.
- Use a physio-roll or underinflated ball.

APENS (1995)
Standard 10.04: Use paraprofessionals and peer tutors for individuals who require greater attention.

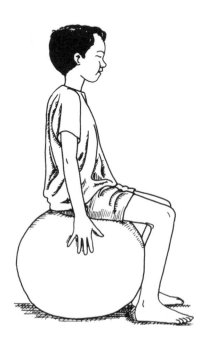 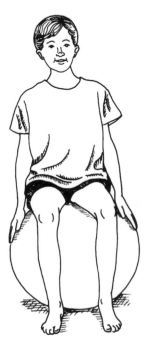 

CHECK STOP

Purpose

To practice stopping quickly on a signal.

Aspect

Coordination.

NASPE Standards (1995)

Standard 5, benchmark for kindergarten: Responds to teacher signal to stop.

Prerequisite Skills

Ability to sit correctly on the ball with balance.

Procedure

Demonstrate while directing students to do the following:

1. Sit on the ball correctly.
2. Begin bouncing gently.
3. Stop bouncing quickly and safely upon hearing the command "Stop!" by leaning forward slightly and holding hands out in front of body, parallel to floor.
4. Practice several times.

Key Points

- Lean slightly forward with upper body and keep feet firmly on floor.
- Place hands in front of body and parallel to the floor as if braking.

Adaptations

- Use a physio-roll or underinflated ball.
- Have paraeducator assist student, according to disability.

APENS (1995)

Standard 10.04: Use paraprofessionals and peer tutors for individuals who require greater attention.

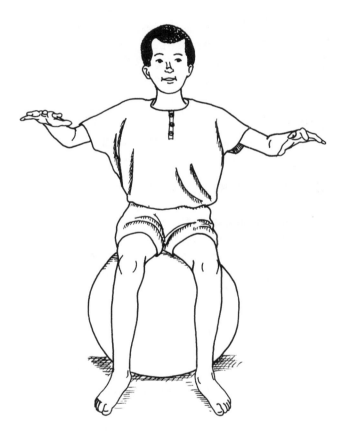

6.3

CLAP

Purpose

To coordinate arm movements with the Basic Bounce.

Aspect

Coordination.

NASPE Standards (1995)

Standard 1, benchmark for kindergarten: Maintains balance while bouncing and clapping hands.

Prerequisite Skills

Ability to do the Basic Bounce.

Procedure

Direct students to do the following:

1. Sit on the ball correctly with hands lightly touching the ball.
2. Clap hands in front of body and return hands to the ball while bouncing.
3. Gradually raise the clapping position until the clap is over the head.

Key Points

- Begin with low claps.
- As control is established, raise clap higher.
- Move arms rhythmically with bounce of the ball.

Variations

- Clap Front and Back: Clap in front of body and then behind.

Adaptations

- Begin with hands in front of body. Clap hands and bring apart. Keep clap small and in front of body.
- Use a physio-roll or underinflated ball.

APENS (1995)

Standard 10.04: Identify and create goal levels for each skill or activity that will allow all individuals with disabilities to achieve levels of success at the same task.

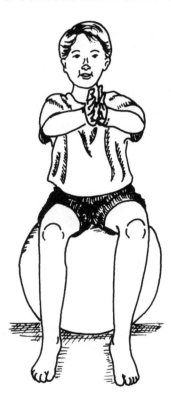

PUSH

Purpose

To coordinate arm movements with the Basic Bounce.

Aspect

Coordination.

NASPE Standards (1995)

Standard 1, benchmark for kindergarten: Maintains balance while bouncing and moving arms.

Prerequisite Skills

Ability to do the Basic Bounce.

Procedure

Direct students to do the following:

1. Start with the hands by the sides, slightly away from the ball.
2. Begin bouncing and raise the elbows about six inches and then push down with the hands, extending the arms and straightening the elbows.
3. Continue to raise the elbows and push down with the hands.

Key Points

- Control the height of the bounce with the size of the push.
- Begin with small pushes and controlled bounces.
- Move arms rhythmically with the bounce of the ball.

Adaptations

- Use a physio-roll or underinflated ball.
- Have paraeducator assist student, according to disability.
- Support student from behind at back and waist.

APENS (1995)

Standard 10.04: Use paraprofessionals and peer tutors for individuals who require greater attention.

LIFT

Purpose

To coordinate arm movements with the Basic Bounce.

Aspect

Coordination.

NASPE Standards (1995)

Standard 1, benchmark for kindergarten: Maintains balance while bouncing and moving arms.

Prerequisite Skills

Ability to do the Basic Bounce.

Procedure

Direct students to do the following:

1. Sit on the ball correctly with hands held above the shoulders, palms upward and elbows bent.
2. Begin bouncing while extending arms and hands toward the ceiling, "pushing" upward.
3. Lower hands to shoulder level and repeat while bouncing.

Key Point

- Begin with small, controlled bounces.

Variation

- Combine with Push (Activity 6.4).

Adaptations

- Use a physio-roll or underinflated ball.
- Have paraeducator assist student, according to disability.

APENS (1995)

Standard 10.04: Use paraprofessionals and peer tutors for individuals who require greater attention.

WINGS

Purpose

To coordinate arm movements with the Basic Bounce.

Aspect

Coordination.

NASPE Standards (1995)

Standard 1, benchmark for kindergarten: Maintains balance while bouncing and moving arms.

Prerequisite Skills

Ability to do the Basic Bounce.

Procedure

Direct students to do the following:

1. Sit on the ball and hold hands (palms down) in front of chest with fingertips almost touching and elbows at shoulder level.
2. Begin bouncing and pull elbows back by squeezing the shoulder blades together.
3. Return to starting position and repeat while bouncing.

Key Points

- Keep elbows high while squeezing shoulder blades together.
- Ensure hands separate to shoulder-width apart when elbows are pulled back.
- Move arms rhythmically with the bounce of the ball.

Adaptations

- Use a physio-roll or underinflated ball.
- Have paraeducator assist student, according to disability.

APENS (1995)

Standard 10.04: Use paraprofessionals and peer tutors for individuals who require greater attention.

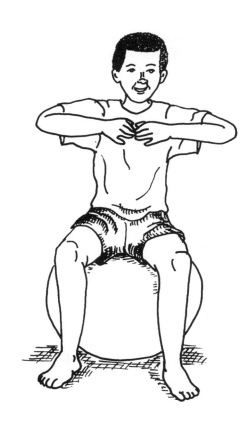

WINDSHIELD WIPERS

Purpose
To coordinate arm movements with the Basic Bounce.

Aspect
Coordination.

NASPE Standards (1995)
Standard 1, benchmark for kindergarten: Maintains balance while bouncing and moving arms.

Prerequisite Skills
Abiltity to do the Basic Bounce.

Procedure
Direct students to do the following:

1. Sit on the ball correctly and hold hands in front of chest as if pressing on a window.
2. Begin moving hands back and forth (left and right) like windshield wipers.

Key Points
- Move arms rhythmically with the bounce of the ball.

Variations
- Rainbow: Make large, inverted U-shaped movements with hands (like a rainbow). *Caution*: The larger movements raise the student slightly off the ball. Begin with small "rainbows" and gradually make larger.

Adaptations
- Use a physio-roll or underinflated ball.

- Have paraeducator assist student, according to disability.

APENS (1995)
Standard 10.04: Use paraprofessionals and peer tutors for individuals who require greater attention.

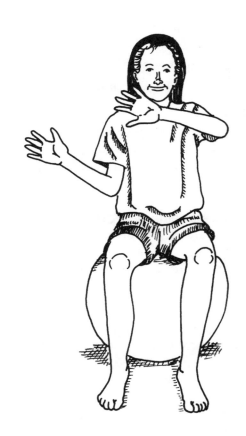

ARM SWINGS

Purpose

To coordinate arm movements with the Basic Bounce.

Aspect

Coordination.

NASPE Standards (1995)

Standard 1, benchmark for kindergarten: Maintains balance while bouncing and moving arms.

Prerequisite Skills

Ability to do the Basic Bounce.

Procedure

Direct students to do the following:

1. Sit on the ball correctly with arms at sides, lightly touching the ball.
2. Begin bouncing and swing one arm forward and the other arm backward.
3. Alternate swinging arms forward and backward while bouncing rhythmically.

Key Points

- Keep arms straight.
- Begin with small movements and gradually make them larger.

Variations

- Symmetrical Arm Swings: Bring arms forward to shoulder height and back down at the same time.
- Runner Arms: Hold arms with elbows near sides, bent at 90-degree angles. Curl hands slightly. Begin bouncing and move arms as in running, bringing the elbow back on one arm and the hand forward on the other.

Adaptations

- Use a physio-roll or underinflated ball.
- Have paraeducator assist student, according to disability.
- Use smaller movements that approximate the form described.

APENS (1995)

Standard 10.04: Identify and create goal levels for each skill or activity that will allow all individuals with disabilities to achieve levels of success at the same task.

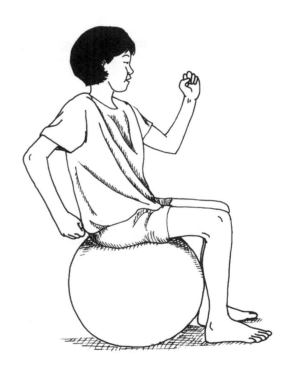

SHOULDER TAPS

Purpose

To coordinate arm movements with the Basic Bounce.

Aspect

Coordination.

NASPE Standards (1995)

Standard 1, benchmark for second grade: Balances, demonstrating momentary stillness, in symmetrical and asymmetrical shapes on a variety of body parts.

Prerequisite Skills

Ability to do the Basic Bounce.

Procedure

Direct students to do the following:

1. Sit on the ball correctly with hands on shoulders.
2. Begin bouncing and extend arms sideways at shoulder level by reaching out with the hands.
3. Return hands to shoulders and continue bouncing while extending and bending arms.

Key Points

- Move rhythmically and keep shoulders relaxed. Movement is in two counts: out/in.

Variations

- Reach-Up: Reach hands upward (above shoulders) and then return hands to shoulders.
- "L" Arms: Reach one arm up and one arm out, then return to shoulders. Alternate the "L" left and right.

Adaptations

- Use a physio-roll or underinflated ball.

- Have paraeducator assist student, according to disability.
- Do arm moves in four counts instead of two.

APENS (1995)

Standard 6.06: Use simple to complex skills.

Reach-Up

ARM RAISES

Purpose
To coordinate arm movements with the Basic Bounce.

Aspect
Coordination.

NASPE Standards (1995)
Standard 1, benchmark for kindergarten: Maintains balance while bouncing and moving arms.

Prerequisite Skills
Ability to do the Basic Bounce.

Procedure
Direct students to do the following:
1. Sit on the ball correctly with hands on thighs.
2. Begin bouncing and raise arms in front to shoulder level.
3. Return hands to thighs.
4. Repeat.

Key Points
- Move rhythmically.
- Keep arms straight.
- Do not lock elbows.

Variations
- Half Jack Arms: Begin with hands at sides, lightly touching the ball. Raise arms sideways to shoulder level and down in rhythm with bouncing.
- Jack Arms: Raise arms sideways and clap lightly overhead.
- Four-Count Jack Arms: Count one—arms shoulder level; count two—hands overhead; count three—arms shoulder level; count four—hands on the ball.

Adaptations
- Use a physio-roll or underinflated ball.
- Have paraeducator assist student, according to disability.
- Do arm moves in four counts instead of two.

APENS (1995)
Standard 6.06: Use simple to complex skills.

Jack Arms

ARM PUNCHES

Purpose

To coordinate arm movements with the Basic Bounce.

Aspect

Coordination.

NASPE Standards (1995)

Standard 1, benchmark for kindergarten: Maintains balance while bouncing and moving arms.

Prerequisite Skills

Ability to do the Basic Bounce.

Procedure

Direct students to do the following:

1. Sit on the ball correctly with elbows at sides and arms bent at 90-degree angles.
2. Punch right arm forward at shoulder level, and return to start.
3. Repeat with left arm.

Key Points

- Move rhythmically with the bounce of the ball.

Variations

- Upward Arm Punches: Punch arm diagonally upward, then return to start.
- Bow and Arrow Arms: Start with hands in front of chest, elbows shoulder-high. Begin bouncing, then extend one arm forward while pulling the other elbow back as in archery. Repeat, extending other arm and pulling opposite arm backward.

Adaptations

- Use a physio-roll or underinflated ball.
- Have paraeducator assist student, according to disability.
- Do arm moves without bouncing.

APENS (1995)

Standard 10.04: Identify and create goal levels for each skill or activity that will allow all individuals with disabilities to achieve levels of success at the same task.

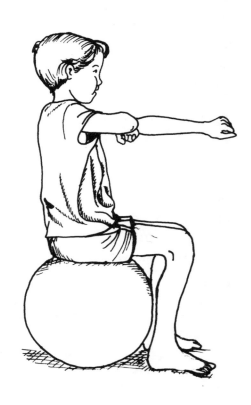

SWIMMING STROKES

Purpose
To coordinate arm movements with the Basic Bounce.

Aspect
Coordination.

NASPE Standards (1995)
Standard 1, benchmark for second grade: Maintains dynamic balance in symmetrical and asymmetrical shapes.

Prerequisite Skills
Ability to do the Basic Bounce.

Procedure
Direct students to do the following:

1. Breaststroke: Demonstrate the breaststroke, being sure to keep arm movements symmetrical, stroking forward from the center of the chest and pulling back to start.
2. Perform while seated bouncing on the ball.

Key Points
- Reach forward with arms while rising on the ball.
- Pull arms back when relaxing downward.

Variations
- Do front crawl.
- Do back crawl.
- Do butterfly.

Adaptations
- Use a physio-roll or underinflated ball.
- Have paraeducator assist student, according to disability.
- Do the arm moves in two or four counts, allowing challenged students more time to accomplish the task.

APENS (1995)
Standard 10.04: Identify and create goal levels for each skill or activity that will allow all individuals with disabilities to achieve levels of success at the same time.

Front Crawl

The foot coordination activities repeat many of the foot activities in chapter 5; now, however, students move their feet while bouncing on the ball. Here are some safety tips to help your students ease into bouncing while moving their feet:

Begin bouncing slowly with small amplitude bounces.

Practice the Check Stop (see Activity 6.2) so students can stop quickly if they start to lose balance.

Maintain control by moving one foot by itself first for eight repetitions and then moving the other foot for eight repetitions. Reduce the number of repetitions to four, then two. The next progression in coordination and balance is to move the feet alternately.

Do jumps *only* when students have practiced the other foot moves successfully.

6.13

SINGLE-FOOT MOVES

Purpose

To coordinate foot moves with the Basic Bounce.

Aspect

Coordination.

NASPE Standards (1995)

Standard 1, benchmark for second grade: Maintains balance while bouncing on the ball and moving feet in a variety of ways.

Prerequisite Skills

Ability to do arm coordination moves while bouncing on the ball.

Procedure

Direct students to do the following:

1. Sit on the ball and begin bouncing.
2. Repeat foot and leg moves from chapter 5:

   - Side Toe Touch (Activity 5.6)
   - Front Toe Touch (variation of Activity 5.12)
   - Heels Apart and Together (variation of Activity 5.4)
   - Front Heel Touch (variation of Activity 5.6)

   - Sideways Heel Touch (variation of Activity 5.12)

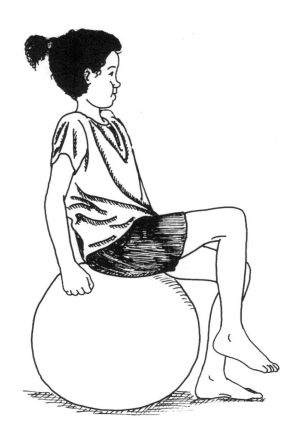

Key Points

- Begin bouncing slowly with small bounces.
- Practice the Check Stop (Activity 6.2) before doing foot moves.
- Maintain control by moving one foot and keeping the other in contact with the floor.
- Begin with eight repetitions, then perform four repetitions, then two.
- Alternate feet only when students demonstrate control with previous single-foot moves.
- Move rhythmically with the bounce of the ball.

Variations

- Step-Around: Take one step to the side of the ball. Close other foot to the first. Continue to move feet in a step-close pattern while turning in a circle on the ball. After turning a full circle, repeat in the other direction.

Adaptations

- Use a physio-roll or underinflated ball.
- Have paraeducator assist student, according to disability.
- Do the foot moves to two or four counts, allowing challenged students more time to accomplish the task.

APENS (1995)

Standard 10.04: Identify and create goal levels for each skill or activity that will allow all individuals with disabilities to achieve levels of success at the same time.

6.14

JUMPING FOOT MOVES—UP AND DOWN

Purpose

To coordinate foot moves with the Basic Bounce.

Aspect

Coordination.

NASPE Standards (1995)

Standard 1, benchmark for second grade: Maintains balance while bouncing on the ball and moving feet in jump patterns.

Prerequisite Skills

Ability to do single-foot moves.

Procedure

Direct students to do the following:

1. Sit on the ball correctly and begin bouncing.
2. Jump feet in place.
3. Use low, controlled bounces and low jumps.

Key Points

- Ensure students demonstrate single-foot moves successfully before attempting any jumping moves.
- Practice the Check Stop before attempting these jump moves.

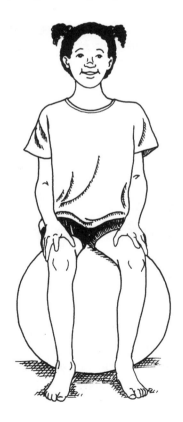

- Lightly hold ball when first practicing these moves.
- Begin bouncing slowly with small bounces.

Variations
- Use the jumping moves in Activity 5.7, Side Straddle, and its variations, Forward and Back Straddle, Skier, and Bell.
- Jump-Around: Move in a circle around the ball by making small jumps.

Adaptations
- Use a physio-roll or underinflated ball.
- Have paraeducator assist student, according to disability.

APENS (1995)
Standard 6.06: Adapt equipment.

Standard 10.04: Use paraprofessionals and peer tutors for individuals who require greater attention.

Activities Combining Hands and Feet

Once students have practiced the hand and foot coordination activities separately and successfully, you may teach students to combine hand and foot movements.

6.15

ARM AND FOOT COMBINATIONS

Purpose
To coordinate arm and foot moves simultaneously with the Basic Bounce.

Aspect
Coordination.

NASPE Standards (1995)
Standard 1, benchmark for fourth grade: Maintains balance while moving arms and feet in a coordinated manner.

Prerequisite Skills
Ability to do coordination arm and foot moves separately.

Procedure
Direct students to do the following:
1. Repeat foot activities and lightly pat the ball with hands.
2. Pat thighs while doing foot moves.
3. Add finger snaps to foot moves.
4. Add clapping to foot moves.

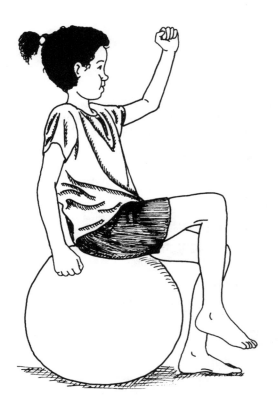

Key Points

- Always begin with low bounces.
- Use single-foot moves first, which keep one foot in contact with the floor.
- Move rhythmically with the bounce of the ball.

Variations

- Use any of the pats while marching.
- Combine Arm Swings and Runner Arms (Activity 6.8 and variation) with marching.
- Use the swimming strokes (Activity 6.12) with the toe moves.
- Perform the heel moves (Activity 5.12) while holding the arms to the side, in front, or overhead.
- Alternate lifting and lowering arms using the opposite arm and foot.
- Do jumping jack coordination exercises by combining Jack Arms (variation of Activity 6.10) and toe or heel moves (Activity 5.12).

CHAPTER 7

RHYTHM AND DANCE

Rhythm is developed through coordination activities. In fact, it is almost impossible when working on the ball to separate balance, coordination, and rhythm as students develop all three abilities while using the ball. In this chapter, we will focus on the rhythmic component. We will discuss beat competency and activities that develop it, describe dance activities we have adapted for use on the ball, and explore creative movement ideas and activities.

Beat Competency

Beat competency is the "ability to express a steady beat" (Weikart 1985). The activities in this section will help students develop a feel for beat and basic timing while moving. They are prerequisites to developing rhythmic competency and other movement success. It is helpful if students have had previous experience with these activities without the ball and if they have mastered starting and stopping—another important part of establishing a sense of basic timing and beat. As with the coordination activities in chapter 6, it is important to practice the Check Stop.

We have adapted some of Phyllis Weikart's activities and suggestions from *Round the Circle* (1987) and *Movement Plus Music* (1985). A three-step progression in developing beat competency progresses from simplest to most complex (Weikart 1985). Through these activities, students practice feeling the beat of the movement and develop tactile kinesthetic decoding (the ability to do the movement), visual decoding (the ability to imitate movement), and aural decoding (the ability to follow verbal directions). How can the ball develop so many areas at once? Bouncing on the ball gives vital feedback to the body, thereby developing a kinesthetic feel for beat. Use music with a strong, steady beat. The beat should be 90 to 110 beats per minute. We often use the *Rhythmically Moving Music* by Phyllis Weikart.

THREE-STEP PROGRESSION

Purpose
To develop beat competency.

Aspect
Rhythm.

NASPE Standards (1995)
Standard 1, benchmark for second grade: Combines patterns in time to music.

Prerequisite Skills
Ability to do the Basic Bounce.

Procedure
Adapted from Phyllis Weikart's *Movement Plus Music* (1985).

Direct students to do the following:

1. Tap the chosen body part (just like the Thigh Pat in Activity 6.1).
2. Tap the chosen body part and say the name of the body part.
3. Repeat steps 1 and 2 with music.

Key Points
- Sit on the ball correctly.
- Use small bounces.
- Use large body parts first (e.g., head, chest, arms, waist).
- Tap softly.
- Move rhythmically with the bounce of the ball.

Adaptations
- Use a physio-roll or underinflated ball.
- Have paraeducator assist student, according to disability.

APENS (1995)
Standard 6.06: Use simple to complex skills. Use multisensory approach, such as providing tactile, kinesthetic, and vestibular input at the same time.

BEAT COMPETENCY PATTERNS

Purpose

To introduce the four patterns of beat competency.

Aspect

Rhythm.

NASPE Standards (1995)

Standard 1, benchmark for second grade: Combines patterns in time to music.

Prerequisite Skills

Ability to do the Basic Bounce.

Procedure

Adapted from Phyllis Weikart's *Movement Plus Music* (1985).

Using the Three-Step Progression described in Activity 7.1, teach students the four patterns of beat competency:

1. Pattern One: Both Hands Simultaneously

   a. Choose one body part (i.e. head) and tap with both hands at the same time for 16 counts. Repeat for 16 counts and say, "head, head, head. . . ." Practice with music.

   b. Then perform the tap with the music and say the name of the body part. Choose another body part and repeat the progression.

2. Pattern Two: One Hand–Other Hand

   a. Choose one body part and tap with one hand for eight counts, then with the other hand for eight counts. For example, tap the right hand on the right thigh, then the left hand on the left thigh.

   b. Repeat and say the name of the body part.

   c. Repeat steps *a* and *b* with music.

   d. Choose another body part and repeat the progression.

3. Pattern Three: Alternate Hands

   a. Choose one body part (e.g., chest) and tap first with one hand, then the other hand, alternating hands on each beat for 16 beats.

   b. Repeat and say the name of the body part.

   c. Repeat steps *a* and *b* with music.

   d. Choose another body part and repeat the progression.

4. Pattern Four: Sequencing Movement

   Work to decrease response time while changing body parts.

   a. Choose two body parts (e.g., chest and thighs). Tap, for example, the chest four times with both hands, then the thighs four times. Next, pat the chest two times and the thighs two times. Then, pat the chest once and the thighs once.

   b. Repeat and say the name of the body parts.

   c. Repeat steps *a* and *b* with music.

   d. Choose another two body parts and repeat the progression.

Key Points

- Sit on the ball correctly.
- Use small bounces.
- Use large body parts first (e.g., head, chest, arms, waist).
- Tap softly.
- Teach the four patterns in order from simple to complex.
- Move rhythmically with the bounce of the ball.

Variations

- Vary the chosen body parts to be tapped as students gain proficiency.

Adaptations

- Use a physio-roll or underinflated ball.
- Have paraeducator assist student, according to disability.

APENS (1995)

Standard 6.06: Use simple to complex skills. Use multisensory approach such as providing tactile, kinesthetic, and vestibular input at the same time.

Determining the Tempo of Music

The tempo of music can be determined several ways. The first is to look at aerobic tapes as they usually list the tempo. Another method is to use a metronome. Set the tempo at 120 beats per minute. Play the music and tap your foot to the beat of the music. If the beat of the music and the foot taps coincide, then the music is the appropriate beat. A third way is to take the beat of the music by counting foot taps for 15 seconds and multiplying by four to get the beats per minute. After working with the ball and music for some time, you will intuitively know if a new piece of music will work. Simply sit on the ball and bounce with the beat to decide if it's appropriate.

7.3

HEAD WAKE-UP

Purpose

To develop beat competency.

Aspect

Rhythm.

NASPE Standards (1995)

Standard 1, benchmark for second grade: Combines patterns in time to music.

Prerequisite Skills

Ability to do the Basic Bounce.

Procedure

Direct students to do the following:

1. Sit on the ball correctly.
2. Begin with Pattern One and tap the top of the head.
3. Add the forehead, cheeks, nose, lips, chin, ears, and back of head.

Key Points

- Sit on the ball correctly.
- Tap softly.
- Use Pattern One, Two, or Three.
- On count eight, call out the next head part.
- Move rhythmically with the bounce of the ball.

Variations

- Try with eyes closed. Tell students to open their eyes if they start to fall.

Adaptations

- Use a physio-roll or underinflated ball.
- Have paraeducator assist student, according to disability.

APENS (1995)

Standard 6.06: Use simple to complex skills. Use multisensory approach such as providing tactile, kinesthetic, and vestibular input at the same time.

RHYMES

Purpose

To develop beat competency.

Aspect

Rhythm.

NASPE Standards (1995)

Standard 1, benchmark for second grade: Combines patterns in time to chant.

Prerequisite Skills

Ability to do the Basic Bounce.

Procedure

Direct students to do the following:

1. Sit on the ball correctly.
2. Begin bouncing on the ball.
3. Establish the beat by saying "bounce" while bouncing.
4. Begin the rhyme immediately after chanting the word "bounce."

Key Points

Sit on the ball correctly.

- Use small bounces.
- Use familiar rhymes such as "Jack and Jill," "Hickory, Dickory, Dock," or "Humpty Dumpty."

Variations

- Use any rhyme or poem.
- Use heart poems from the American Heart Association's *HeartPower* (AHA, 1996) for example:

Day and night, night and day.

My heart is always pumping away.

It doesn't pause, it doesn't stop

It pushes my blood from bottom to top.

Out, around, back and then

It starts to do it all over again.

Night and day, day and night

My heart keeps pumping with all its might.

Adaptations

- Chant the rhymes at a slower rate.
- Use underinflated ball or physio-roll.
- Have paraeducator assist student, according to disability.

APENS (1995)

Standard 6.06: Use simple to complex skills. Use multisensory approach such as providing tactile, kinesthetic, and vestibular input at the same time.

1-2-3-4

Purpose

To develop beat competency.

Aspect

Rhythm.

NASPE Standards (1995)

Standard 1, benchmark for second grade: Combines patterns in time to music.

Prerequisite Skills

Ability to do the Basic Bounce.

Procedure

Adapted from Rae Pica and Richard Gardzina's *Let's Move and Learn* (1990).

Direct students to do the following:

1. Start with the Basic Bounce.
2. Establish the beat by saying "bounce" while bouncing.
3. Begin the music.

Count for four beats (listen, bounce and count 1-2-3-4); repeat.

Clap for four beats; repeat (listen; bounce and clap; listen and repeat).

Step for four beats; repeat (listen; bounce and march; listen and repeat).

Rest for four beats; repeat (listen and sit still; listen and repeat).

Count two; clap two; repeat (listen; bounce and count twice, clap twice; listen and repeat).

Clap two; step two; repeat (listen; bounce and clap twice, march twice; listen and repeat).

Step two; rest two; repeat (listen; bounce and march twice, rest for two counts; listen and repeat).

Count one; clap three; repeat (listen; bounce and count to one, clap to three; listen and repeat).

Clap one; step three; repeat (listen; bounce and clap once, march three steps; listen and repeat).

Step one; rest three; repeat (listen; bounce and march one step, then rest for three counts; listen and repeat).

Count three; clap one; repeat (listen; bounce and count to three, clap once; listen and repeat).

Clap three; step one; repeat (listen; bounce and clap three times, march one step; listen and repeat).

Step three; rest one; repeat (listen; bounce and march three times, rest once; listen and repeat).

Key Points

- Sit on the ball correctly.
- Use small bounces.
- Choose music with four beats to a measure.
- Match the movement to each beat.
- Stop on signal.
- Separate the decoding process by doing the following: listen first (auditory), do the action (kinesthetic), listen and do the same action.
- "Rest" means no movement and count to yourself.

Adaptations

- Address only part of the song in a lesson (e.g., do only verses that have the same action for four beats, such as count for four beats).
- Use a physio-roll or underinflated ball.
- Have paraeducator assist student, according to disability.

APENS (1995)

Standard 6.06: Use simple to complex skills. Use multisensory approach such as providing tactile, kinesthetic, and vestibular input at the same time.

THE FREEZE

Purpose
To develop beat competency.

Aspect
Rhythm.

NASPE Standards (1995)
Standard 5, benchmark for kindergarten: Can start and stop on signal.

Prerequisite Skills
Ability to do the Basic Bounce, to stop and start, and freeze while standing.

Procedure
Direct students to do the following:

1. Sit on the ball correctly.
2. Begin bouncing on the ball.
3. Establish the beat by saying, "bounce," while bouncing.
4. When the music is playing, bounce on the ball or model teacher's coordination actions (e.g., alternate arm swings, shoulder taps).
5. Stop when the music stops.
6. Begin bouncing again when the music starts.

Key Points
- Sit on the ball correctly.
- Use small bounces.
- Begin bouncing when the music starts.
- Practice the Check Stop.

Variations
Include movement concepts and creative dance:
- Move elbows and feet.
- Move arms at medium level.
- Keep arms straight or bent.
- Move feet lightly or on tiptoes.
- Move feet heavily, like a giant dinosaur.
- Lift the ball and turn with it.
- Drop and stop the ball or dribble it.
- On "Freeze!" pose in any shape while remaining in contact with the ball. Add movement concepts: curve arms, keep legs straight, support weight on stomach, put hands at high level, face backward.

Adaptations
- Just bounce instead of adding coordination activities.
- Model the teacher's actions until movement vocabulary is large enough to create new movements.
- Use a physio-roll or underinflated ball.
- Have paraeducator assist student, according to disability.

APENS (1995)
Standard 6.06: Use simple to complex skills. Provide games that involve body shape imitation.

Rhythmic competency is the ability to coordinate movement with time. The rhythmically competent student can match an external beat with a physical task. Success with rhythmic movement activities results through experiencing a sequence of interrelated and increasingly complex rhythmic coordination activities. The accurate timing and coordinated movement of skillful performers both require rhythmic competency.

The ball is an essential addition to the development of rhythmic competency. The compression of the ball by the user and the rebound sets up a perpetual rhythmic motion helping the learner move her body in coordinated ways. Total body bouncing along with using the arms and legs, separately or combined, create meaningful rhythmic experiences. Students can control the rate of the bounce by themselves or to music. Finally, rhythmic coordination activities not only improve rhythmic ability, they also reinforce the concept of beat. Music by Rae Pica and Richard Gardzina works well for these activities.

7.7

THE BODY SONG

Purpose

To develop rhythmic competency.

Aspect

Rhythm.

NASPE Standards (1995)

Standard 1, benchmark for second grade: Combines patterns in time to music.

Prerequisite Skills

Ability to do the Basic bounce.

Procedure

From Rae Pica and Richard Gardzina's *Let's Move & Learn* (1990).

Direct students to do the following:

1. Sit on the ball correctly.
2. Begin bouncing on the ball.
3. Establish the beat by saying "bounce" while bouncing.
4. Begin the song:

Show me you can touch your toes, (change "toes" to "clothes," bounce at the same time)

Then bring your hand up to your nose; (bounce and bring both hands to nose)

Put a smile upon your face, (bounce and smile)

Do it all in your own space! (bounce and check out space)

Chorus: The body, the body! (eight bounces)

      What parts do you know? (eight bounces)

      The body, the body, (eight bounces)

Touch it high and low! (on the word "high" stretch both hands over head; on the word "low" drop hands to side of ball)

Bring your elbows to your knees, (just do the action without bouncing)

Then shake all over if you please. (shake as many body parts as possible while remaining balanced on the ball)

Straighten up with hands on hips, (bounce with hands on hips)

Can you pucker up those lips? (bounce and pucker)

Chorus: Touch your ankle with your hand, (change ankle to "leg," "kneecap," or "shin")

Upon one foot can you now stand? (pick up one foot and remain balanced on the ball)

Wiggle fingers in the air, (bounce and hold hands up)

Shake your hips now, if you dare. (do the hula)

Chorus: Close your eyes, then open them quick, (can they bounce at the same time?)

Around your lips let your tongue lick, (bounce and lick)

With your shoulders you can shrug, (bounce and shrug)

Give yourself a great big hug! (bounce and hug)

Key Points

- Sit on the ball correctly.
- Use small bounces.
- Begin with Pattern One (both hands simultaneously) for developing beat competency.
- During the chorus bounce, tap body parts or try any of the coordination activities from chapter 6.

Variations

- Use the other beat competency patterns.

Adaptations

- Try the actions first without bouncing.
- Change body parts to be touched to those that are more accessible (e.g., "toes" to "clothes").
- Use a physio-roll or underinflated ball.
- Have paraeducator assist student, according to disability.

APENS (1995)

Standard 6.06: Use simple to complex skills. Use multisensory approach such as providing tactile, kinesthetic, and vestibular input at the same time.

7.8

MACARENA (LATIN AMERICA)

Purpose

To develop rhythmic competency.

Aspect

Rhythmic movement.

NASPE Standards (1995)

Standard 1, benchmark for second grade: Combines patterns in time to music.

Prerequisite Skills

Ability to do the Macarena sitting or standing on floor.

Procedure

Direct students to do the following:

1. Begin seated on the ball correctly.
2. Perform the dance as follows:

Count	Movement
1	Extend right arm forward, palm down.
2	Extend left arm forward, palm down.
3	Turn right hand, palm up.
4	Turn left hand, palm up.
5	Place right hand on left shoulder.
6	Place left hand on right shoulder.
7	Place right hand on back of head.
8	Place left hand on back of head.

Count	Movement
9	Place right hand on left hip.
10	Place left hand on right hip.
11	Place right hand on right hip.
12	Place left hand on left hip.
13	Sway hips gently like the hula (no bouncing).
14	Continue hula (no bouncing).
15	Step to the side with right foot.
16	Close left foot to right and turn one-quarter.

Key Points

- Review movements without music.
- Do not bounce during counts 13 and 14 (hula).

Variations

- Have young children perform the dance as follows:

Count	Movement
1-2	Extend both arms forward, palms down.
3-4	Extend both arms forward, palms up.
5-6	Place both hands on shoulders.
7-8	Place both hands on back of head.

Count	Movement
9-10	Place both hands on hips.
11-12	Both hands remain on hips.
13-14	Sway both hips gently like the hula.
15-16	Clap twice (or rest two counts).

Adaptations

- Use a physio-roll or underinflated ball.
- Have paraeducator assist student, according to disability.

APENS (1995)

Standard 6.06: Adapt equipment.

Standard 10.04: Use paraprofessionals and peer tutors for individuals who require greater attention.

HOKEY POKEY (USA)

Purpose
To develop rhythmic competency.

Aspect
Rhythmic movement.

NASPE Standards (1995)
Standard 1, benchmark for second grade: Combines patterns in time to music.

Prerequisite Skills
Ability to do the Hokey Pokey while sitting or standing on floor and the coordination activities on the ball (chapter 6).

Procedure
Direct students to do the following:

1. Sit on the ball correctly.
2. Begin bouncing.
3. Perform usual moves for the Hokey Pokey (e.g., put your right hand in, put your right hand out . . .).
4. On the chorus, stand and with one hand lightly touching the ball, walk around the ball, and wave the other hand above the head.

Key Points
- Sit on the ball correctly.
- Use small bounces.
- Move rhythmically with the bounce of the ball.

Variations
- For young children, begin with Pattern One (Both Hands Simultaneously). Separate the decoding process, that is, demonstrate motions without talking. On the chorus, bounce and wave hands at head level.

Adaptations
- Use a physio-roll or underinflated ball.
- Have paraeducator assist student, according to disability.

APENS (1995)
Standard 6.06: Adapt equipment.

Standard 10.04: Use paraprofessionals and peer tutors for individuals who require greater attention.

THE WHEELS ON THE BUS

Purpose
To develop rhythmic competency.

Aspect
Rhythm.

NASPE Standards (1995)
Standard 1, benchmark for second grade: Combines patterns in time to rhyme, song or music.

Prerequisite Skills
Basic Bounce, arm coordination activities.

Procedure
Direct students to do the following:

1. Sit on the ball.
2. Begin bouncing on the ball.
3. Establish the beat by saying, "bounce," while doing the action of bouncing.
4. Begin the song immediately after chanting the word, "bounce."

The wheels on the bus go round and round, round and round, round and round. The wheels on the bus go round and round, all through the town.

Roll one arm over the other in front of body while bouncing on the ball.

The wipers on the bus go swish, swish swish, swish, swish, swish, swish, swish. The wipers on the bus go swish, swish, swish, all through the town.

Both hands are held in front of the body at face level and both move to the right and down, then left, while bouncing on the ball.

The doors on the bus go open and shut, open and shut, open and shut. The doors on the bus go open and shut, all through the town.

Arms are bent at right angles with elbows held at shoulder level. Open arms to sides of body on the word "open," then together in front of body on the word "shut," while bouncing on the ball.

Key Points:

- Sit on the ball correctly.
- Use small bounces.
- Use the familiar tune and words to the song of "Wheels On The Bus."

Variations

- Additional verses from the song.
- Suggestions from your students. (What else moves on the bus? What do people do on the bus?)

Adaptations

- Sing the song at a slower rate.
- Use a physio-roll or underinflated ball.
- Paraeducator assists student according to disability.

APENS (1995)

Standard 6.06: Use simple to complex skills. Provide games that involve body shape imitation.

SEVEN JUMPS (DANISH)

Purpose
To develop rhythmic competency.

Aspect
Rhythmic movement.

NASPE Standards (1995)
Standard 1, benchmark for second grade: Balances, demonstrating momentary stillness, in symmetrical and asymmetrical shapes on a variety of body parts.

Prerequisite Skills
Ability to balance on the ball and do Seven Jumps while sitting or standing on floor.

Procedure
Direct students to do the following:

1. Sit on the ball correctly.
2. Begin the song:

Begin bouncing for 16 counts.

Pause and pose for 2 counts: Touch knees, then hips.

Bounce for 16 counts.

Pause and pose for 3 counts: Touch knees, hips, and add elbows.

Bounce for 16 counts.

Pause and pose for 4 counts and pose: Add touch of shoulders.

Bounce for 16 counts.

Pause and pose for 5 counts: Add touch of head.

Bounce for 16 counts.

Pause and pose for 6 counts: Add arm extension overhead.

Bounce for 16 counts.

Pause and pose for 7 counts: Add picking up one foot.

Bounce for 16 counts.

Pause and pose for 8 counts: Add picking up other foot.

Bounce for 16 counts.

Key Points
- Sit on the ball correctly.
- Move smoothly, slowly, and with control.
- Use small bounces.
- Teacher begins as the leader.
- Sequence eight different poses throughout the dance.
- Hold each pose as still as possible.
- Note this dance allows response time.
- Move rhythmically with the bounce of the ball.

Variations
- Creative Movement: Allow students to demonstrate different poses. Make a list of eight new poses each time the dance is performed.

Adaptations
- Use a physio-roll or underinflated ball.
- Have paraeducator assist student, according to disability.

APENS (1995)

Standard 6.06: Adapt equipment.

Standard 10.04: Use paraprofessionals and peer tutors for individuals who require greater attention.

7.12

ALLEY CAT (USA)

Purpose

To develop rhythmic competency.

Aspect

Rhythmic movement.

NASPE Standards (1995)

Standard 1, benchmark for second grade: Combines patterns in time to music.

Prerequisite Skills

Ability to balance on the ball and do the Alley Cat while sitting or standing on floor.

Procedure

Direct students to do the following:

1. Sit on the ball correctly.
2. Perform dance as follows:

Count	Movement
1-8	Touch right foot to the right side and back in place twice, then left foot to the left twice.
9-16	Touch right foot back and in place two times, then left foot back two times.
17-24	Raise right knee and touch the floor two times, then left knee two times.
25-28	Raise right knee once, then left knee once.
29-32	Step to the right one quarter turn, close left foot to the right and clap.

Key Points

- Sit on the ball correctly.
- Do the dance without bouncing.

Variations

- Add bouncing.

Adaptations

- Use a physio-roll or underinflated ball.
- Have paraeducator assist student, according to disability.

APENS (1995)

Standard 6.06: Adapt equipment.

Standard 10.04: Use paraprofessionals and peer tutors for individuals who require greater attention.

POPCORN (USA)

Purpose

To develop rhythmic competency.

Aspect

Rhythmic movement.

NASPE Standards (1995)

Standard 1, benchmark for second grade: Combines patterns in time to music.

Prerequisite Skills

Ability to balance on the ball and do the Popcorn while sitting or standing on floor.

Procedure

Direct students to do the following:

1. Sit on the ball correctly.
2. Perform the dance as follows:

Count	Movement	Count	Movement
1-8	Touch right heel forward and back; repeat. Touch left heel forward and back; repeat.	17-24	Kick right foot out, then touch floor; repeat. Kick left foot out, then touch floor; repeat.
9-16	Raise right knee up, then down; repeat. Raise left knee up, then down; repeat.	25-32	Rock to the right for two counts, then to the left two counts; repeat.

Key Points

- Sit on the ball correctly.
- Do the dance without bouncing.

Variations

- Add bouncing.

Adaptations

- Touch the foot (versus only the heel) out to the front.
- Say "Kick one foot out, now kick the other foot out," instead of "right" or "left."
- Use a physio-roll or underinflated ball.
- Have paraeducator assist student, according to disability.

APENS (1995)

Standard 6.06: Adapt equipment.

Standard 10.04: Use paraprofessionals and peer tutors for individuals who require greater attention.

DJURKJEVKA (YUGOSLAVIA)

Purpose
To develop rhythmic competency.

Aspect
Rhythmic movement.

NASPE Standards (1995)
Standard 1, benchmark for second grade: Combines patterns in time to music.

Prerequisite Skills
Ability to balance on the ball and do the Djurkjevka while sitting or standing on floor.

Procedure
Direct students to do the following:

1. Sit on the ball correctly.
2. Perform the dance as follows:

Count	Movement	Count	Movement
1-8	Walk in place: right, left, right, left, right, left, stamp three times—right, right, right.	17-24	Touch right toe forward, to the side and in place, hold one count. Repeat with left foot.
9-16	Repeat starting with left foot.	25-32	Repeat toe touch.

Key Points
- Sit on the ball correctly.
- Do the dance without bouncing.

Variations
- Add bouncing.

Adaptations
- Touch the foot (instead of the toe) out to the front.
- Say "one foot, then the other," instead of "right" or "left."
- Use a physio-roll or underinflated ball.
- Have paraeducator assist student, according to disability.

APENS (1995)
Standard 6.06: Adapt equipment.

Standard 10.04: Use paraprofessionals and peer tutors for individuals who require greater attention.

ERSKO KOLO (YUGOSLAVIA)

Purpose
To develop rhythmic competency.

Aspect
Rhythmic movement.

NASPE Standards (1995)
Standard 1, benchmark for second grade: Combines patterns in time to music.

Prerequisite Skills
Ability to balance on the ball and do the Ersko Kolo while sitting or standing on floor.

Procedure
Direct students to do the following:
1. Sit on the ball correctly.
2. Perform the dance as follows:

Count	Movement	Count	Movement
1-8	Do Side Straddle (Activity 5.7) two times.	21-24	March left, right, left, right.
9-16	Do Forward and Back Straddle (variation of Activity 5.7) two times.	25-28	Kick forward left, right, left, right.
17-20	Kick forward right, left, right, left.	29-32	March right, left, right, left.

Key Points
- Sit on the ball correctly.
- Do the dance without bouncing.

Variations
- Add bouncing.

Adaptations
- Use easier foot movements or jumps.
- Say "kick one foot out, now kick the other foot out," instead of "right" or "left."
- Use a physio-roll or underinflated ball.
- Have paraeducator assist student, according to disability.

APENS (1995)
Standard 6.06: Adapt equipment.

Standard 10.04: Use paraprofessionals and peer tutors for individuals who require greater attention.

BELE KAWE (AFRICAN)

Purpose

To develop rhythmic competency.

Aspect

Rhythmic movement.

NASPE Standards (1995)

Standard 1, benchmark for second grade: Combines patterns in time to music.

Prerequisite Skills

Ability to balance on the ball and do the Bela Kawa while sitting or standing on floor.

Procedure

Direct students to do the following:

1. Sit on the ball correctly.
2. Hold arms at shoulder level, bend elbows so hands are at head level (goalpost arms).
3. Perform the dance as follows:

Count	Movement
1-8	Step to the side with right foot (open), then step left foot to right foot (close). Repeat to the left. Repeat each side. Arms sway to the right and left with the foot touches.
9-16	Touch right heel forward, then step in place. Repeat with left heel. Repeat each side. Hands gently touch the ball or are placed on hips.

Count	Movement
17-24	Stand and place right hand lightly on the ball and walk slowly around the ball.
25-32	Repeat with left hand on the ball.

Key Points

- Sit on the ball correctly.
- Do the dance without bouncing.

Variations

- Add bouncing.

Adaptations

- Do foot movements only.
- Say "touch one foot forward, then the other," instead of "right" or "left."
- Bounce or step around ball while seated during counts 17 through 32.
- Use a physio-roll or underinflated ball.
- Have paraeducator assist student, according to disability.

APENS (1995)

Standard 6.06: Adapt equipment.

Standard 10.04: Use paraprofessionals and peer tutors for individuals who require greater attention.

The Swiss Balls can stimulate the imagination and provide fresh alternatives to mundane activities. Scott Liebler's *Jungle Walk* (1992) inspired us to start thinking of all the different movements that could be acted out on the ball. Students can do creative movements while sitting, prone, or supine. Movements can mimic animals, occupations, leisure-time activities, or fundamental motor skills. Let the students share their many ideas and extensions of creative movement.

Using the balls to act out stories is an excellent way to integrate physical education with other subject areas. The librarian can be a wonderful source in finding movement books. Music teachers may have music, stories, or instruments you can add to creative movement experiences. Classroom teachers can encourage students to dictate, write, or draw movement stories to read in the gym and reenact using the balls.

7.17

MOVEMENT FRAMEWORK

Purpose
To develop manipulative skills, creativity, and self-expression.

Aspect
Manipulation, creativity, movement exploration.

NASPE Standards (1995)
Standard 2, benchmark for kindergarten: Identifies and uses a variety of relationships with objects (e.g., over and under, behind, alongside, through).

Prerequisite Skills
Abililty to do basic movement skills while sitting or standing on the floor.

Procedure
Direct students to do the following:
1. Find a self-space with a ball.
2. Show how many ways you can do the following:

Get the ball behind you?	Get the ball under you?	Get the ball over you?	Roll the ball in a straight line? Circle?
Push the ball?	Rock on the ball?	Balance on the ball?	Curl on the ball?
Make yourself small on the ball?	Stretch on the ball?	Make yourself long on the ball?	Make yourself big on the ball?
Keep just your feet on the ball?	Put your head on the ball?	Put your elbows on the ball?	Make yourself wide on the ball? Narrow?

Keep yourself and their ball in self space?	Move with your ball in general space?	Move forward, backward or sideways with your ball?	Get your ball to high level, medium, or low level?
Do something slow with your ball?	Do something softly and gently?	Do something strong and hard?	Do something on the ball? Off the ball but still touching it?
Move around the ball (touching or not touching)?	Move the ball away from the wall? Toward the wall?	Move the ball with one other person? Two other people?	

Key Points
- Remember safety rules at all times.
- Stay in self-space.
- Be creative—use own ideas, not someone else's.

Adaptations
- Use a physio-roll or underinflated ball.
- Have paraeducator assist student, according to disability.
- Use floor spots.

APENS (1995)
Standard 6.06: Adapt equipment. Use floor spots for "home base."

7.18

FISHING

Purpose
To demonstrate creativity and self-expression while using the ball.

Aspect
Balance, coordination, self-expression, and creativity.

NASPE Standards (1995)
Standard 4, benchmark for kindergarten: Sustains moderate to vigorous physical activity; is aware of his or her heart beating fast during physical activity.

Prerequisite Skills
Ability to perform skills while sitting or standing on the floor, sit on the ball correctly, find pulse, and demonstrate the difference between fast and slow speeds.

Procedure
Direct students to do the following:
1. Sit on the ball correctly.
2. Begin bouncing.
3. Mime fly fishing.
4. Land a fish.
5. Reel in a giant fish, then release it back into the stream.
6. Continue with other related actions, such as casting, getting the line caught and untangling it, responding to a nibble on the line ("tug on the line") or to a bite ("you've got a big one").

Key Points
- Remember safety rules at all times.
- Stay in self-space.

- Be creative—use own ideas, not someone else's.
- Start with a detailed list of creative movement ideas, then allow students to add to it.

Variations
- Use any children's book. Read to students, allowing them to perform movements throughout the story.
- Use resources in appendix E (audio adventure tapes—Silly-Cise, 1992).
- Allow students to make up action stories and act them out on the ball.

Adaptations
- Provide support from behind.

- Use a physio-roll or underinflated ball.
- Have paraeducator assist student, according to disability.
- Use floor spots.

APENS (1995)
Standard 10.01: Design for a variety and modification of equipment in each activity to ensure successful completion of each assigned task. Select tasks that can be performed by the individual with a disability individually and safely. Identify and create goal levels for each skill or activity that will allow all individuals with disabilities to achieve levels of success at the same task.

7.19

BOATING

Purpose
To demonstrate creativity and self-expression while using the ball.

Aspect
Balance, coordination, self-expression, and creativity.

NASPE Standards (1995)
Standard 4, benchmark for kindergarten: Sustains moderate to vigorous physical activity; is aware of his or her heart beating fast during physical activity.

Prerequisite Skills
Ability to perform skills while sitting or standing on the floor, sit on the ball correctly, find pulse, and demonstrate the difference between fast and slow speeds.

Procedure
Direct students to do the following:
1. Sit on the ball in self-space.
2. Begin bouncing.
3. Begin rowing a "boat."
4. Sing "Row, Row, Row Your Boat."
5. Change to a canoe and paddle downstream. Ask "How does this look different from rowing?"

6. Explain details of getting the canoe moving, steering around rocks, and parking the canoe at the riverbank.

Key Points
- Remember safety rules at all times.
- Stay in self-space.
- Be creative—use own ideas, not someone else's.
- Start with a detailed list of creative movement ideas, then allow students to add to it.

Variations
- Use any children's book. Read to students, allowing them to perform movements throughout the story.
- Use resources listed in appendix E (audio adventure tapes—Silly-Cise, 1992).
- Allow students to make up action stories and act them out on the ball.

Adaptations
- Do without bouncing.
- Provide support from behind.
- Use a physio-roll or underinflated ball.
- Have paraeducator assist student, according to disability.
- Use floor spots.

7.20

STATUES

Purpose

To encourage self-expression.

Aspect

Stopping on signal, balance.

NASPE Standards (1995)

Standard 2, benchmark for kindergarten: Identifies and uses a variety of body shapes.

Prerequisite Skills

Ability to stop on signal, make different body shapes, take weight on a variety of body parts, and do the Basic Bounce.

Procedure

Direct students to do the following:

1. Sit on the ball correctly in self-space in circle or random formation.
2. Begin the Basic Bounce.
3. On signal, stop bouncing and make a shape with the body while seated on the ball.
4. Continue, changing to a different shape on each signal.

Key Points

- Be sure to begin in sitting position each time.

- Stay in self-space.
- Keep one body part in contact with the floor.
- Make a shape as soon as possible upon signal.

Variations

- Use supine or prone positions.
- Begin seated on the ball and, on signal, put any body part on the ball to make the statue.
- Use different signals to "freeze": season, number, letter, whistles, music.

- Make a statue with a partner or small group.

Adaptations

- Use a physio-roll or underinflated ball.
- Use floor spots.
- Have paraeducator assist student, according to disability.

APENS (1995)

Standard 6.06: Use floor spots for "home base."

CHAPTER 8

FLEXIBILITY

As you probably know, students rarely see stretching as fun. The ball changes this; because it is so inviting, students willingly participate in exercises that improve the flexibility of all body parts. In the back, the lumbar (low back), thoracic (midback), and cervical (neck) muscles benefit. In the legs, the quadriceps, hip flexors, and hamstrings improve. The side muscles (external obliques and internal obliques) and chest (pectorals) also benefit. Moreover, stretching occurs as a by-product of using the ball in other ways. Repeat Activity 5.4 on the Swiss Ball to introduce how the Swiss Ball can help enhance flexibility. Then use the activities in this chapter to increase this important aspect of health-related fitness.

BACK TWIST

Purpose

To rotate the spine through full range of motion while resting the body on the floor.

Aspect

Flexibility.

NASPE Standards (1995)

Standard 4, benchmark for second grade: Moves each joint through full range of motion.

Prerequisite Skills

Ability to hold the ball.

Procedure

Direct students to do the following:

1. Lie on back with knees bent and feet on the floor.
2. Hold the ball in both hands and lift it up over the chest.
3. Lower the ball to the floor on one side of the body while also lowering knees to the other side. Hold 10 seconds.
4. Return to start.
5. Repeat to the other side.
6. Repeat sequence five times.

Key Points

- Do not move hands on the ball.
- Keep eyes on the ball and allow head to turn to follow it.
- Inhale while lifting; exhale while lowering.
- Keep knees and feet together.

Adaptations

- Only move arms through partial range.
- Only move the arms or the legs.
- Use underinflated ball.
- Have paraeducator assist student, according to disability.

APENS (1995)

Standard 3.03: Emphasize flexibility exercises for individuals.

Standard 6.06: Provide activities that increase pressure on body surfaces, joints, and muscles, such as pushing and pulling.

Standard 10.04: Use paraprofessionals and peer tutors for individuals who require greater attention.

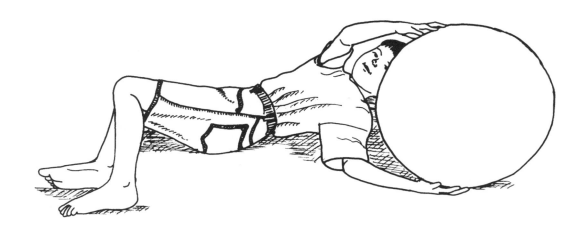

SIDE, BACK, AND SHOULDER STRETCH

Purpose

To expand the rib cage, bend to the side, and rotate the shoulders.

Aspect

Flexibility.

NASPE Standards (1995)

Standard 4, benchmark for second grade: Moves each joint through full range of motion.

Prerequisite Skills

Ability to hold and roll the ball.

Procedure

Direct students to do the following:

1. Sit on the floor in a straddle position with knees slightly bent.
2. Put the ball between legs an arm's length in front and touch it with both hands.
3. Roll the ball slowly to one foot, allowing the spine to bend to the side, and look under armpit.
4. Return to start.
5. Repeat to the other side.
6. Repeat sequence five times.

Key Points

- Do not move hands on the ball.
- Keep head between arms and allow neck to bend to the side.
- Inhale while bending to the side; exhale while returning to center.

Variations

- Kneel behind ball and sit on heels.
- Roll ball from side to side as far as possible.

Adaptations

- Only move through partial range.
- Sit in a chair and put ball on a table in front of student.
- Have paraeducator assist student, according to disability.

APENS (1995)

Standard 3.03: Emphasize flexibility exercises for individuals.

Standard 6.06: Provide activities that increase pressure on body surfaces, joints, and muscles, such as pushing and pulling.

Standard 10.04: Use paraprofessionals and peer tutors for individuals who require greater attention.

TRUNK TWIST

Purpose
To rotate the spine while sitting.

Aspect
Flexibility.

NASPE Standards (1995)
Standard 4, benchmark for second grade: Moves each joint through full range of motion.

Prerequisite Skills
Ability to sit on the ball correctly.

Procedure
Direct students to do the following:

1. Sit on the ball correctly.
2. Raise arms forward to shoulder level with hands shoulder-width apart.
3. Move straight arms around behind body as far as possible, allowing shoulders and head to follow.
4. Return to start.
5. Repeat to the other side.
6. Repeat sequence five times.

Key Points
- Do not move feet.
- Keep ball almost still.
- Inhale while twisting; exhale while returning to center.

Variation
- Hold a weighted ball in between hands.

Adaptations
- Only move through partial range.
- Have paraeducator assist student, according to disability.

APENS (1995)
Standard 3.03: Emphasize flexibility exercises for individuals.

Standard 6.06: Provide activities that increase pressure on body surfaces, joints, and muscles, such as pushing and pulling.

Standard 10.04: Use paraprofessionals and peer tutors for individuals who require greater attention.

LUNGE

Purpose

To rotate the spine and stretch hips and shoulders in a sitting position.

Aspect

Flexibility.

NASPE Standards (1995)

Standard 4, benchmark for second grade: Moves each joint through full range of motion.

Prerequisite Skills

Ability to sit on the ball correctly.

Procedure

Direct students to do the following:

1. Sit on the ball correctly then place feet as far apart as comfortable.
2. Raise arms forward to shoulder level with hands shoulder-width apart.
3. Move straight arms around behind body to one side as far as possible (allowing shoulders and head to follow) while extending knee of opposite leg behind body.
4. Return to start.
5. Repeat to the other side.
6. Repeat sequence five times.

Key Points

- Keep knees in line with feet.
- Keep ball almost still.
- Inhale while twisting; exhale while returning to center.

Variation

- Raise front arm upward to increase stretch.

Adaptations

- Only move through partial range.
- Touch ball with hand on side of rotation.
- Have paraeducator assist student, according to disability.

APENS (1995)

Standard 3.03: Emphasize flexibility exercises for individuals.

Standard 6.06: Provide activities that increase pressure on body surfaces, joints, and muscles, such as pushing and pulling.

Standard 10.04: Use paraprofessionals and peer tutors for individuals who require greater attention.

PRONE STRETCH

Purpose
To relax and elongate the muscles of the spine.

Aspect
Flexibility.

NASPE Standards (1995)
Standard 4, benchmark for second grade: Moves each joint through full range of motion.

Prerequisite Skills
Ability to do the Prone Balance (Activity 5.10).

Procedure
Direct students to do the following:
1. Kneel on floor behind ball and place abdomen over top of ball.
2. Fold hands, placing them on ball, and relax neck till chin rests on ball.
3. Allow ball to roll slightly forward, relaxing body weight onto ball.

Key Points
- Do not let ball roll over hands or long hair.
- Inhale while rolling forward; exhale while returning to center.

Variations
- Dig toes into floor, pushing to rock body forward and relaxing to rock backward to increase stretch.
- Rock side to side.
- Rocking Push-Up: In the rocking position, with hands on the floor, have students rock forward and touch their noses lightly to the floor. Then using arms, push back to feet and knees. Repeat 10 times. This is a great weight-assisted beginning push-up that students delight in being able to do.

Adaptations
- Only move through partial range.
- Touch hands to floor.
- Have paraeducator assist student, according to disability.

APENS (1995)
Standard 3.03: Emphasize flexibility exercises for individuals.

Standard 6.06: Provide activities that increase pressure on body surfaces, joints, and muscles, such as pushing and pulling.

Standard 10.04: Use paraprofessionals and peer tutors for individuals who require greater attention.

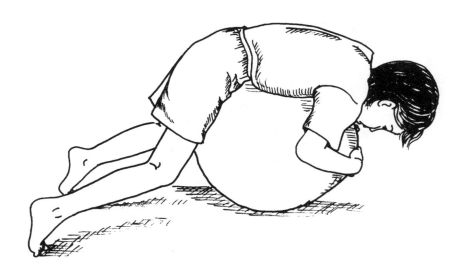

BACK AND SHOULDER STRETCH

Purpose
To stretch shoulder and midspine flexor muscles.

Aspect
Flexibility.

NASPE Standards (1995)
Standard 4, benchmark for second grade: Moves each joint through full range of motion.

Prerequisite Skills
Ability to kneel behind ball.

Procedure
Direct students to do the following:

1. Kneel behind ball and place hands on top of ball with arms extended.
2. Sit down on heels and allow spine to relax and curve forward.
3. Roll ball forward, allowing hips to rise slightly, keeping chest low to the floor.
4. Hold stretch at end of range before returning to start.

Key Points
- Move hands on ball as it rolls forward so arms remain straight.
- Keep head between arms and eyes focused on floor.
- Inhale while rolling forward; exhale while returning to center.

Variations
- When spine is extended to end of range, roll ball side to side.
- Allow feet to lift off floor to extend spine further, then roll ball side to side.

Adaptations
- Only move through partial range.
- Have student sit in a chair and put ball on a table in front of student.
- Have paraeducator assist student, according to disability.

APENS (1995)
Standard 3.03: Emphasize flexibility exercises for individuals.

Standard 6.06: Provide activities that increase pressure on body surfaces, joints, and muscles, such as pushing and pulling.

Standard 10.04: Use paraprofessionals and peer tutors for individuals who require greater attention.

SIDE STRETCH

Purpose
To relax and elongate rib cage and lateral muscles of the spine.

Aspect
Flexibility.

NASPE Standards (1995)
Standard 4, benchmark for second grade: Moves each joint through full range of motion.

Prerequisite Skills
Ability to do the Back and Shoulder Stretch on the ball.

Procedure
Direct students to do the following:
1. Kneel next to ball, placing outside leg out to side and hands on top of ball.
2. Lie sideways over top of ball and let top arm hang overhead.
3. Press top foot into floor, allowing body to roll over ball sideways.
4. Relax weight of body on ball and keep body in line so only side touches ball.
5. Hold at end of range before returning to start.

Key Points
- Provide a spotter for a student's first attempt. Spotter should stand to side and put hands on student's waist.
- Keep feet planted on floor once knees start to extend.
- Inhale while rolling sideways; exhale while returning to center.

Variations
- Gently rock in end position.

Adaptations
- Only move through partial range.
- Touch the floor with bottom hand for balance.
- Have student sit in a chair and put ball on a low table next to student.
- Have paraeducator assist student, according to disability.

APENS (1995)
Standard 3.03: Emphasize flexibility exercises for individuals.

Standard 6.06: Provide activities that increase pressure on body surfaces, joints, and muscles, such as pushing and pulling.

Standard 10.04: Use paraprofessionals and peer tutors for individuals who require greater attention.

BACK ARCH

Purpose

To relax and elongate the muscles that flex the hips, spine, and shoulders.

Aspect

Flexibility.

NASPE Standards (1995)

Standard 4, benchmark for second grade: Moves each joint through full range of motion.

Prerequisite Skills

Ability to sit on the ball correctly.

Procedure

Direct students to do the following:

1. Sit on the ball correctly.
2. Walk feet forward while leaning body back onto the ball.
3. Let ball roll up spine to midback as hips sink into a squatting position.
3. Simultaneously straighten knees to roll ball backward and reach arms up overhead till hands touch floor.
4. Hold at end of range before returning to start.

Key Points

- Provide a spotter for a student's first attempt. Spotter should stand to side and put hands on student's waist.
- Keep feet planted on floor once knees start to extend.
- Inhale while rolling backward; exhale while returning.

Variations

- Gently rock in end position.

Adaptations

- Touch ball with hands while walking out for balance.
- Only move through partial range.
- Use physio-roll.
- Have paraeducator assist student, according to disability.

APENS (1995)

Standard 3.03: Emphasize flexibility exercises for individuals.

Standard 6.06: Provide activities that increase pressure on body surfaces, joints, and muscles, such as pushing and pulling.

Standard 10.04: Use paraprofessionals and peer tutors for individuals who require greater attention.

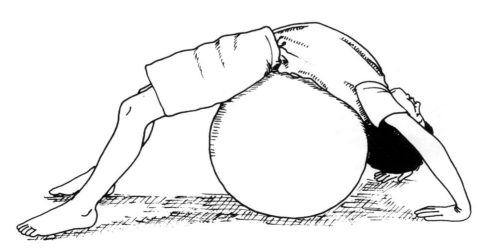

HAMSTRING STRETCH

Purpose
To stretch the hamstrings.

Aspect
Flexibility.

NASPE Standards (1995)
Standard 4, benchmark for second grade: Moves each joint through full range of motion.

Prerequisite Skills
Ability to follow directions.

Procedure
Direct students to do the following:

1. Lie on back on floor.
2. Place the ball under knees and relax.
3. Straighten one knee and lift leg up till foot is over hip.
4. Flex ankle by stretching toes toward body.
5. Hold for count of 10.
6. Return to start.
7. Repeat sequence with other leg.

Key Points
- Keep hips and back flat on floor.
- Do not hold breath; breathe comfortably.

Variations
- Sit on ball, place feet forward so knees are straight, and bend forward at hips, keeping spine straight.

Adaptations
- Only move through partial range.
- Have paraeducator assist student, according to disability.

APENS (1995)
Standard 3.03: Emphasize flexibility exercises for individuals.

Standard 10.04: Use paraprofessionals and peer tutors for individuals who require greater attention.

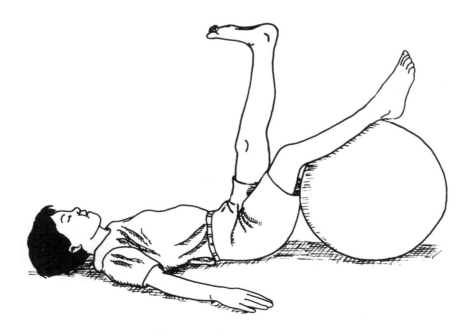

PIRIFORMIS STRETCH

Purpose

To stretch the piriformis muscle that externally rotates the hip.

Aspect

Flexibility.

NASPE Standards (1995)

Standard 4, benchmark for second grade: Moves each joint through full range of motion.

Prerequisite Skills

Ability to follow directions.

Procedure

Direct students to do the following:

1. Lie on back on floor.
2. Place ball under knees and straighten them.
3. Bend one knee and place ankle on other leg right above knee.
4. Roll ball toward body by bending straight leg.
5. Hold for count of 10.
6. Return to start.
7. Repeat sequence on other side.

Key Points

- Keep back flat on floor.
- Do not hold breath; breathe comfortably.

Adaptations

- Only move through partial range.
- Have paraeducator assist student, according to disability.

APENS (1995)

Standard 3.03: Emphasize flexibility exercises for individuals.

Standard 10.04: Use paraprofessionals and peer tutors for individuals who require greater attention.

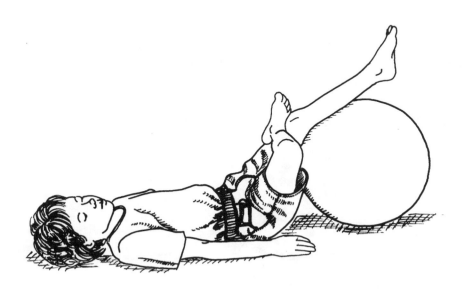

HIP FLEXOR STRETCH

Purpose
To stretch the hip flexor muscle (iliopsoas).

Aspect
Flexibility.

NASPE Standards (1995)
Standard 4, benchmark for second grade: Moves each joint through full range of motion.

Prerequisite Skills
Ability to do the Prone Balance (Activity 5.10).

Procedure
Direct students to do the following:

1. Kneel on floor behind ball and place hands on top of ball.
2. Bring one foot as far forward next to the ball as possible.
3. Place elbows on top of ball, allowing body weight to rest on ball.
4. Roll ball forward, keeping back knee on floor till stretch is felt.
5. Hold for count of 10.
6. Return to start.
7. Repeat sequence on other side.

Key Points
- Keep front knee in line with toes.
- Do not allow knee to pass over toes.
- Do not hold breath; breathe comfortably.

Variations
- Dig back toe into floor and straighten knee off floor to increase stretch.
- Rock forward and backward.

Adaptations
- Allow trunk to rest fully on ball and touch hands to the floor.
- Only move through partial range.
- Have paraeducator assist student, according to disability.

APENS (1995)
Standard 3.03: Emphasize flexibility exercises for individuals.

Standard 6.06: Provide activities that increase pressure on body surfaces, joints, and muscles, such as pushing and pulling.

Standard 10.04: Use paraprofessionals and peer tutors for individuals who require greater attention.

QUADRICEPS STRETCH

Purpose

To stretch the quadriceps (knee extensors).

Aspect

Flexibility.

NASPE Standards (1995)

Standard 4, benchmark for second grade: Moves each joint through full range of motion.

Prerequisite Skills

Ability to do the Tabletop Balance (Activity 5.15).

Procedure

Direct students to do the following:

1. Begin in Tabletop Balance.
2. Slide one foot backward toward the ball as far as possible.
3. Keep toes on floor, allowing heel to lift and knee to drop toward floor till stretch is felt.
4. Hold for count of 10.
5. Return to start.
6. Repeat sequence on other side.

Key Points

- Allow hands to touch floor for balance.
- Keep hips lifted to maintain Tabletop Balance.
- Do not hold breath; breathe comfortably.

Adaptations

- Only move through partial range.
- Touch hands to ball while getting to Tabletop Balance.
- Use physio-roll.
- Have paraeducator assist student, according to disability.

APENS (1995)

Standard 3.03: Emphasize flexibility exercises for individuals.

Standard 6.06: Provide activities that increase pressure on body surfaces, joints, and muscles, such as pushing and pulling.

Standard 10.04: Use paraprofessionals and peer tutors for individuals who require greater attention.

CHAPTER 9

MUSCULAR STRENGTH AND CARDIORESPIRATORY FITNESS

The Swiss Ball is an excellent piece of equipment for helping students develop muscular strength and cardiovascular fitness. The fun of using the ball increases student motivation and enhances each workout. The Swiss Ball is also a very appropriate and safe way to introduce elementary students to fitness activities in general. In this chapter, we'll present both cardiovascular fitness and muscular strength activities on the ball.

Muscular Strength

You can use the ball to develop muscular strength either with or without resistance bands. Use the variations provided with each activity to increase difficulty or create variety. We'll describe 10 activities using the ball only, then share 13 activities that include the resistance band.

ABDOMINAL CURL

Purpose
To strengthen the abdominal muscles (rectus abdominus).

Aspect
Strength.

NASPE Standards (1995)
Standard 4, benchmark for fourth grade: Engages in appropriate activity that results in development of muscular strength.

Standard 4, benchmark for sixth grade: Correctly demonstrates activities designed to improve and maintain muscular strength and endurance, flexibility, cardiorespiratory functioning, and proper body composition.

Procedure
Direct students to do the following:
1. Lie on back with knees bent and feet on floor.
2. Hold ball on stomach with both hands.
3. Roll ball up thighs to top of knees while lifting head and shoulders off floor and allowing spine to curl.
4. Hold for count of 10.
5. Return to start.
6. Repeat five times.

Key Points
- Keep chin a fist's distance from chest.
- Exhale while lifting; inhale while lowering.

Variations
- Abdominal Curl With Obliques: Hold ball on stomach with one hand and put other hand behind head. Then, roll ball diagonally up thighs with hand to top of opposite knee while lifting head and shoulder off floor and allowing spine to curl diagonally. Be sure to keep elbow of hand behind head on floor. Repeat to other side.

Adaptations
- Only move through partial range.
- Support head with one hand for Abdominal Curl.
- Have paraeducator assist student, according to disability.

APENS (1995)
Standard 6.06: Provide activities that increase pressure on body surfaces, joints, and muscles, such as pushing and pulling. Use a multisensory approach such as providing tactile, kinesthetic, and vestibular input at the same time.

ABDOMINAL ROTATION

Purpose

To strengthen the abdominal muscles (internal and external obliques).

Aspect

Strength.

NASPE Standards (1995)

Standard 4, benchmark for fourth grade: Engages in appropriate activity that results in development of muscular strength.

Standard 4, benchmark for sixth grade: Correctly demonstrates activities designed to improve and maintain muscular strength and endurance, flexibility, cardiorespiratory functioning, and proper body composition.

Procedure

Direct students to do the following:

1. Lie on back and place ball under calves with knees bent.
2. Let knees move, rolling ball sideways as far as possible, allowing spine to rotate.
3. Tighten abdominal muscles to return to starting position.
4. Repeat to other side.

Key Points

- Keep back and lower hip on floor and arms at side of body for stability.
- Do not let legs slide off ball.
- Exhale while lifting; inhale while lowering.

Adaptations

- Only move through partial range.
- Have paraeducator assist student, according to disability.

APENS (1995)

Standard 6.06: Provide activities that increase pressure on body surfaces, joints, and muscles, such as pushing and pulling. Teach wide base of support and low center of gravity.

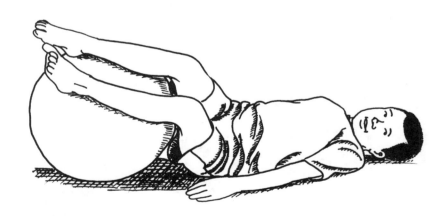

FROG LEGS

Purpose

To strengthen the abdominal, hip, and knee flexor and extensor muscles.

Aspect

Strength.

NASPE Standards (1995)

Standard 4, benchmark for fourth grade: Engages in appropriate activity that results in development of muscular strength.

Standard 4, benchmark for sixth grade: Correctly demonstrates activities designed to improve and maintain muscular strength and endurance, flexibility, cardiorespiratory functioning, and proper body composition.

Prerequisite Skills

Ability to grasp and lift ball between ankles.

Procedure

Direct students to do the following:

1. Lie on back with knees bent and place ball between ankles.
2. Prop up on elbows.
3. Lift ball and bring knees toward chest.
4. Straighten legs out above the floor and return to chest.
5. Repeat.

Key Points

- Do not drop ball.
- Exhale while straightening legs; inhale while bending knees.

Variations

- Lie flat on floor and bend and straighten legs while keeping ball high off floor.

Adaptations

- Only move through partial range or allow ball to roll on floor.
- Perform exercise without a ball.
- Have paraeducator assist student, according to disability.

APENS (1995)

Standard 6.06: Provide activities that increase pressure on body surfaces, joints, and muscles, such as pushing and pulling. Teach wide base of support and low center of gravity.

Frog Legs Without Elbow Lift

SIDE LEG LIFTS

Purpose
To strengthen the hip abductors and adductors.

Aspect
Strength.

NASPE Standards (1995)
Standard 4, benchmark for fourth grade: Engages in appropriate activity that results in development of muscular strength.

Standard 4, benchmark for sixth grade: Correctly demonstrates activities designed to improve and maintain muscular strength and endurance, flexibility, cardiorespiratory functioning, and proper body composition.

Prerequisite Skills
Ability to grasp and lift ball between ankles.

Procedure
Direct students to do the following:

1. Lie on side with legs straight.
2. Place lower hand under head and upper hand in front of body at waist.
3. Place ball between legs at lower calves and ankles and squeeze.
4. Lift ball up off floor by lifting legs up sideways.
5. Slowly lower legs to floor.
6. Repeat 10 times.
7. Repeat sequence on other side.

Key Points
- Do not drop ball.
- Exhale while lifting legs; inhale while lowering.
- Keep body in a straight line.

Adaptations
- Only move through partial range.
- Perform exercise without a ball.
- Have paraeducator assist student, according to disability.

APENS (1995)
Standard 6.06: Provide activities that increase pressure on body surfaces, joints, and muscles, such as pushing and pulling. Teach wide base of support and low center of gravity.

HALF SIT-UP

Purpose
To strengthen the abdominal muscles used for sitting.

Aspect
Strength.

NASPE Standards (1995)
Standard 4, benchmark for fourth grade: Engages in appropriate activity that results in development of muscular strength.

Standard 4, benchmark for sixth grade: Correctly demonstrates activities designed to improve and maintain muscular strength and endurance, flexibility, cardiorespiratory functioning, and proper body composition.

Prerequisite Skills
Ability to sit on the ball correctly.

Procedure
Direct students to do the following:

1. Sit on the ball correctly.
2. Simultaneously raise straight arms overhead, lift heels up, lean backward with body, and let ball roll forward.
3. Hold for a count of 10.
4. Return to start.
5. Simultaneously raise straight arms behind body, rock back on heels, and lean body forward as ball rolls backward.
6. Hold for a count of 10.
7. Return to start.
8. Repeat 10 times.

Key Points
- Keep spine in optimal posture, leaning from the hips.
- Allow ball to roll forward and backward as far as possible while keeping balance.
- Inhale while leaning backward; exhale while leaning forward.

Variations
- Half Sit-Up With Obliques: After step 6 in the Half Sit-Up, lower one arm to outside of opposite knee. Hold for a count of 10. Raise arm back up overhead. Repeat with other arm. Exhale while lowering arm; inhale while raising arm.

Adaptations
- Cross arms over chest for Half Sit-Up.
- Do not fully extend arms and keep feet flat for Half Sit-Up With Obliques.
- Only move through partial range.
- Use a physio-roll or underinflated ball.
- Have paraeducator assist student, according to disability.

APENS (1995)
Standard 2.01: Implement activities that stimulate upright postures and control of head, neck, and trunk.

Standard 6.06: Use a multisensory approach such as providing tactile, kinesthetic, and vestibular input at the same time.

TABLETOP WALK-OUT

Purpose

To strengthen the muscles that support the spine.

Aspect

Strength.

NASPE Standards (1995)

Standard 4, benchmark for fourth grade: Engages in appropriate activity that results in development of muscular strength.

Standard 4, benchmark for sixth grade: Correctly demonstrates activities designed to improve and maintain muscular strength and endurance, flexibility, cardiorespiratory functioning, and proper body composition.

Prerequisite Skills

Ability to do the Tabletop Balance (Activity 5.22).

Procedure

Direct students to do the following:

1. Sit on the ball correctly.
2. Walk feet forward while leaning backward, allowing ball to roll up spine until upper back and neck rest on ball.
3. Raise straight arms up overhead to form straight line with the trunk.
4. Hold for a count of 10.
5. Slowly return to starting position.

Key Points

- Do not arch back or let hips sag down.
- Do not hold breath; breathe comfortably.

Variations

- Keep feet on floor and shift weight from one side to the other.
- Pick up one foot and straighten knee.

Adaptations

- Clasp hands behind head for support or touch hands to floor for balance.
- Only move through partial range.
- Use a physio-roll or underinflated ball.
- Have paraeducator assist student, according to disability.

APENS (1995)

Standard 6.06: Use a multisensory approach such as providing tactile, kinesthetic, and vestibular input at the same time.

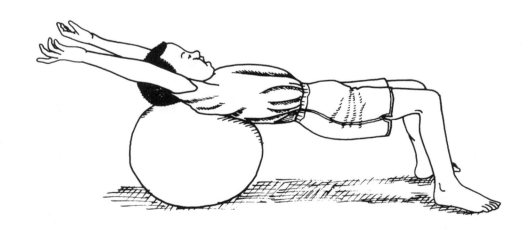

BASIC BRIDGING

Purpose

To strengthen hip and spine extensor muscles.

Aspect

Strength.

NASPE Standards (1995)

Standard 4, benchmark for fourth grade: Engages in appropriate activity that results in development of muscular strength.

Standard 4, benchmark for sixth grade: Correctly demonstrates activities designed to improve and maintain muscular strength and endurance, flexibility, cardiorespiratory functioning, and proper body composition.

Procedure

Direct students to do the following:

1. Lie on back and place legs on ball and straight arms on floor at sides for support.
2. Straighten legs and raise buttocks off floor to form straight line from shoulders to feet.
3. Hold for a count of 10.
4. Slowly lower body to floor one vertebra at a time.

Key Points

- Do not arch back or let hips sag down.
- Inhale while lifting; exhale while lowering.

Variations

- Place ball further down legs.
- Lift one leg off ball.
- Lift one leg and write the alphabet with the foot.
- Bridging With Bent Elbows: Instead of keeping arms straight, bend elbows, pointing fingers toward ceiling. Use first three variations with this variation as well.
- Bridging With Raised Arms: When students master Bridging With Bent Elbows, have them lift straight arms off floor, parallel to body. Use first three variations with this variation as well.

Adaptations

- Place ball closer to buttocks.
- Only move through partial range.
- Use a physio-roll or underinflated ball.
- Have paraeducator assist student, according to disability.

APENS (1995)

Standard 6.01: Adapt fitness activities to individuals with low motor skills.

Standard 6.06: Teach wide base of support and low center of gravity.

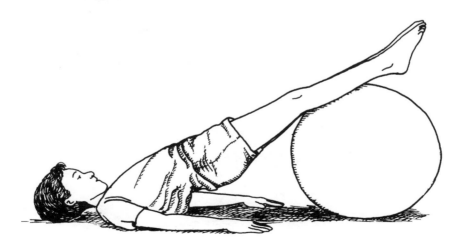

BACK EXTENSION

Purpose

To strengthen back extensor muscles against gravity.

Aspect

Strength.

NASPE Standards (1995)

Standard 4, benchmark for fourth grade: Engages in appropriate activity that results in development of muscular strength.

Standard 4, benchmark for sixth grade: Correctly demonstrates activities designed to improve and maintain muscular strength and endurance, flexibility, cardiorespiratory functioning, and proper body composition.

Prerequisite Skills

Ability to do Prone Balance.

Procedure

Direct students to do the following:

1. Kneel behind ball and place stomach and chest on top.
2. Place hands behind head and raise elbows out to side.
3. Lift head, neck, and upper back until back is straight.
4. Hold for a count of 10.
5. Slowly return to starting position.

Key Points

- Avoid arching back or neck by keeping lower ribs on ball.
- Inhale while lifting; exhale while lowering.

Variations

- Hold arms out to sides and lift up trunk.
- Dig toes into floor and extend knees, then lift one leg off floor. Repeat with other leg.
- Lift one leg and write the alphabet with the foot. Repeat with other leg.

Adaptations

- Only lift through partial range.
- Use a physio-roll or underinflated ball.
- Have paraeducator assist student, according to disability.

APENS (1995)

Standard 6.01: Adapt fitness activities to individuals with low motor skills.

Standard 6.06: Teach wide base of support and low center of gravity.

PRONE WALK-OUT

Purpose

To strengthen arm, shoulder, and trunk muscles surrounding the spine.

Aspect

Strength.

NASPE Standards (1995)

Standard 4, benchmark for fourth grade: Engages in appropriate activity that results in development of muscular strength.

Standard 4, benchmark for sixth grade: Correctly demonstrates activities designed to improve and maintain muscular strength and endurance, flexibility, cardiorespiratory functioning, and proper body composition.

Prerequisite Skills

Ability to do the Prone Balance (Activity 5.17).

Procedure

Direct students to do the following:

1. Kneel behind ball and place stomach and chest over ball, letting hands touch the floor.
2. Walk hands forward, allowing ball to roll under body to knees.
3. Hold for a count of 10.
4. Slowly return to starting position.

Key Points

- Keep head and body aligned and eyes focused on floor. Do not let back sag.
- Do not hold breath; breathe comfortably.

Variations

- Walk out until ball is under ankles.
- Gently roll ball side to side or front to back.
- Lift one leg and write the alphabet with the foot. Repeat with other leg.
- Prone Push-Up: Begin in Prone Walk-Out position and bend elbows to lower nose to floor. Then, straighten arms, keeping body in a straight line. Inhale while bending elbows; exhale while straightening. Do as many as possible. To make harder, lift one leg, increase speed, or put feet on floor and hands on ball.
- Prone Knee Curl: Begin in Prone Walk-Out position with knees on top of ball. Moving slowly with control, lift hips and bend knees, allowing ball to roll forward underneath trunk until shins rest on ball. Relax trunk in full flexion before straightening knees and hips to return to start. Inhale while body flexes; exhale while body extends. Repeat 10 times. Student may need to readjust position of

knees on top of ball after a few repetitions. To vary further, increase speed of reps or have another student hold ankles and walk along to resist movement.

Adaptations

- For Prone Walk-Out and Prone Push-Up, only walk out to hips or thighs.
- Have students spot each other by assisting balance at waist.
- Use a physio-roll or underinflated ball.
- Have paraeducator assist student, according to disability.

- Only move through partial range for Prone Push-Up and Prone Knee Curl.

APENS (1995)

Standard 6.01: Adapt fitness activities to individuals with low motor skills.

Standard 6.06: Provide activities that increase pressure on body surfaces, joints, and muscles, such as pushing and pulling.

Standard 10.01: Design activities that allow students to work together in pairs.

9.10

HAMSTRING CURL

Purpose

To strengthen hamstring muscles.

Aspect

Strength.

NASPE Standards (1995)

Standard 4, benchmark for fourth grade: Engages in appropriate activity that results in development of muscular strength.

Standard 4, benchmark for sixth grade: Correctly demonstrates activities designed to improve and maintain muscular strength and endurance, flexibility, cardiorespiratory functioning, and proper body composition.

Prerequisite Skills

Ability to do Basic Bridging.

Procedure

Direct students to do the following:

1. Lie down on back, place soles of feet on the ball, and bend knees.
2. Lift hips to bridge position, keeping knees bent (as in Basic Bridging).
3. Allowing ball to roll, slowly let knees straighten, then bend knees and roll the ball toward buttocks.
4. Repeat.

Key Points

- Raise hips till shoulders and knees are aligned.
- Do not bend knees further if muscle cramping is felt; instead, straighten knee immediately.
- Do not hold breath; breathe comfortably.

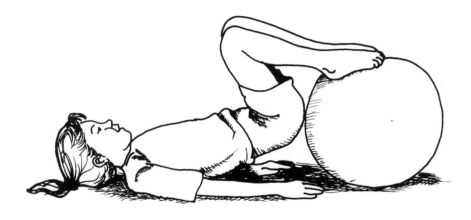

Variations

- Perform bridge with one leg. Repeat with other leg.
- Bridge up with one leg and roll ball by straightening and bending that leg. Repeat with other leg.

Adaptations

- Only move through partial range of motion.

- Use a physio-roll or underinflated ball.
- Have paraeducator assist student, according to disability.

APENS (1995)

Standard 6.06: Teach wide base of support and low center of gravity. Provide activities that increase pressure on body surfaces, joints, and muscles, such as pushing and pulling.

9.11

HALF SQUAT

Purpose

To strengthen hip and knee extensor muscles and teach proper body mechanics for lifting.

Aspect

Strength.

NASPE Standards (1995)

Standard 4, benchmark for fourth grade: Engages in appropriate activity that results in development of muscular strength.

Standard 4, benchmark for sixth grade: Correctly demonstrates activities designed to improve and maintain muscular strength and endurance, flexibility, cardiorespiratory functioning, and proper body composition.

Prerequisite Skills

Ability to stand and lift ball in front of body with hands.

Procedure

Direct students to do the following:

1. Stand in optimal posture with feet hip-width apart.
2. Hold ball in front of body with elbows bent at right angles.
3. Push ball away from body by straightening arms while bending hips and knees to Half Squat position.
4. Hold for a count of five.
5. Slowly return to starting position.

Key Points

- Keep spine aligned and bend only at hips.
- Inhale while squatting; exhale while straightening.
- Keep hips over knees during squat.

Variations

- Take one step forward while squatting.
- Wall Squat: Stand in front of a wall and place the ball behind waist between the back and the wall. Bend knees and hips and reach toward floor until in a Half Squat position while allowing ball to roll up the spine. Keep knees over feet while bending knees. Hold for a count of five. Slowly straighten to starting position. To increase difficulty, lift one foot while squatting. Repeat with other foot.

Adaptations

- Spread feet wider apart to give a larger base of support.
- Only move through partial range.
- Perform exercise without a ball.
- Have paraeducator assist student, according to disability.

APENS (1995)

Standard 2.01: Structure tasks and activities to stimulate and facilitate normal postural responses.

Standard 10.02: Teach the correct form to perform the skill.

9.12

PRONE SHOULDER FLEXION

Purpose

To strengthen shoulder flexors and back extensors in prone position using resistance band.

Aspect

Strength.

NASPE Standards (1995)

Standard 4, benchmark for fourth grade: Engages in appropriate activity that results in development of muscular strength.

Standard 4, benchmark for sixth grade: Correctly demonstrates activities designed to improve and maintain muscular strength and endurance, flexibility, cardiorespiratory functioning, and proper body composition.

Prerequisite Skills

Ability to do the Prone Balance (Activity 5.17).

Procedure

Direct students to do the following:

1. Kneel behind ball.
2. Place stomach on the ball and hands on floor in front of the ball.
3. Grasp the resistance band with both hands shoulder-width apart.
4. Place weight on one hand, keeping elbow straight.
5. Lift free straight arm overhead to shoulder level.
6. Slowly return to starting position.
7. Repeat five times with first arm.
8. Repeat five times with other arm.

Key Points

- Relax body weight on the ball.
- Keep head aligned with spine and eyes focused on floor.
- Move smoothly, slowly, and with control so band does not snap.
- Keep wrists straight to resist the band.
- Inhale while lifting; exhale while lowering.

Variations

- Leg Extension: To incorporate the whole body and challenge balance skills, dig toes into the floor and straighten knees so they come off the floor (may use with next two variations as well).

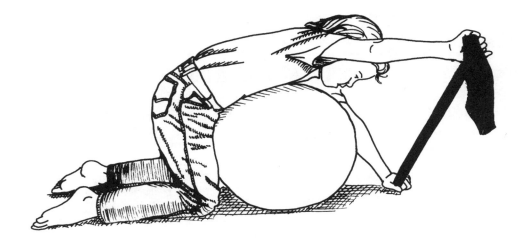

Prone Shoulder Extension

- Prone Shoulder Extension: Once weight has been placed on one hand (step 4), instead of lifting free straight arm overhead to shoulder level, pull free straight arm alongside body, bringing hand to hip.
- Prone Shoulder Abduction: To also strengthen shoulder and scapula abductors. Once weight has been placed on one hand (step 4), instead of lifting free straight arm overhead to shoulder level, pull free hand out sideways to shoulder level, keeping arm straight.

Adaptations

- Have paraeducator assist student, according to disability.

- The paraeducator can spot for balance by holding student at waist.
- Use a band with more elasticity and less resistance.
- Perform exercise without a resistance band.
- Adapt range of motion as necessary.
- Allow free arm to bend for Prone Shoulder Abduction.

APENS (1995)

Standard 3.03: Emphasize strength-training programs for hypotonic individuals.

Standard 6.06: Provide activities that increase pressure on body surfaces, joints, and muscles, such as pushing and pulling.

HORIZONTAL ARM PULL

Purpose
To strengthen shoulder abductor muscles and spine extensors using a resistance band.

Aspect
Strength.

NASPE Standards (1995)
Standard 4, benchmark for fourth grade: Engages in appropriate activity that results in the development of muscular strength.

Standard 4, benchmark for sixth grade: Correctly demonstrates activities designed to improve and maintain muscular strength and endurance, flexibility, cardiorespiratory functioning, and proper body composition.

Prerequisite Skills
Ability to sit on the ball correctly.

Procedure
Direct students to do the following:

1. Sit on the ball correctly.
2. Properly grasp resistance band.
3. Hold band shoulder-width apart at shoulder level.
4. Keeping elbows straight, pull arms apart, stretching band to the chest.
5. Slowly return to starting position.
6. Repeat five times.

Key Points
- Maintain optimal posture.
- Tighten abdominal muscles.
- Inhale while stretching; exhale while relaxing.
- Keep wrists straight.

Variations
- Perform exercise with one foot raised off floor.

- Arm Pull-Down: To also strengthen scapula abductor and shoulder adductor muscles. Hold band overhead shoulder-width apart instead of at shoulder level. Pull hands apart and down behind head, lowering to shoulder level. To vary further, keep arms straight or raise one foot off floor. Repeat, raising other foot off floor.

Adaptations
- Lower height of arms.
- Use only one arm.
- Use lighter resistance band or no band.
- Use a physio-roll or underinflated ball.
- Have paraeducator assist student, according to disability

APENS (1995)
Standard 3.03: Emphasize strength-training programs for hypotonic individuals.

Standard 10.02: Teach the correct form necessary to perform the skill.

HORIZONTAL CHEST PRESS

Purpose

To strengthen elbow extensor muscles (triceps) and scapula protractor muscles using a resistance band.

Aspect

Strength.

NASPE Standards (1995)

Standard 4, benchmark for fourth grade: Engages in appropriate activity that results in the development of muscular strength.

Standard 4, benchmark for sixth grade: Correctly demonstrates activities designed to improve and maintain muscular strength and endurance, flexibility, cardiorespiratory functioning, and proper body composition.

Prerequisite Skills

Ability to sit on the ball correctly.

Procedure

Direct students to do the following:

1. Sit on the ball correctly.
2. Properly grasp resistance band, approximately shoulder width apart.
3. Raise band overhead and then down around back.
4. Hold the band at chest level with elbows bent to start.
5. Push hands forward at shoulder level until arms are straight.
6. Slowly return to starting position.
7. Repeat five times.

Key Points

- Maintain optimal posture.
- Tighten abdominal muscles.
- Inhale while stretching; exhale while relaxing.
- Keep wrists straight.

Variations

- Alternate arms.
- Perform exercise with one foot raised off floor. Repeat with other foot.

Adaptations

- Use a physio-roll or underinflated ball.
- Have paraeducator assist student, according to disability.
- Lower height of arms.
- Use only one arm.
- Use lighter resistance band or no band.

APENS (1995)

Standard 3.03: Emphasize strength-training programs for hypotonic individuals.

Standard 6.06: Provide activities that increase pressure on body surfaces, joints, and muscles, such as pushing and pulling.

VERTICAL TRICEPS PRESS

Purpose

To strengthen the elbow extensors (triceps) using a resistance band.

Aspect

Strength.

NASPE Standards (1995)

Standard 4, benchmark for fourth grade: Engages in appropriate activity that results in the development of muscular strength.

Standard 4, benchmark for sixth grade: Correctly demonstrates activities designed to improve and maintain muscular strength and endurance, flexibility, cardiorespiratory functioning, and proper body composition.

Prerequisite Skills

Ability to sit on the ball correctly.

Procedure

Direct students to do the following:

1. Sit on the ball correctly.
2. Properly grasp resistance band shoulder-width apart.
3. Place one hand on opposite shoulder with other hand directly below bent at about a 90-degree angle.
4. Straighten lower elbow and allow hand to pass behind side of body.
5. Slowly return to starting position, keeping band taut.
6. Repeat five times.
7. Repeat sequence with other arm.

Key Points

- Maintain optimal posture.
- Tighten abdominal muscles.
- Inhale while stretching; exhale while relaxing.
- Keep wrists straight.

Variations

- Perform exercise with one foot raised off floor. Repeat with other foot.

Adaptations

- Use a physio-roll or underinflated ball.
- Have paraeducator assist student, according to disability.
- Only extend elbow through partial range.
- Use lighter resistance band or no bands.

APENS (1995)

Standard 3.03: Emphasize strength-training programs for hypotonic individuals.

Standard 6.06: Provide activities that increase pressure on body surfaces, joints, and muscles, such as pushing and pulling.

SHOULDER FLEXION

Purpose

To strengthen shoulder flexor muscles and spine extensors using a resistance band.

Aspect

Strength.

NASPE Standards (1995)

Standard 4, benchmark for fourth grade: Engages in appropriate activity that results in the development of muscular strength.

Standard 4, benchmark for sixth grade: Correctly demonstrates activities designed to improve and maintain muscular strength and endurance, flexibility, cardiorespiratory functioning, and proper body composition.

Prerequisite Skills

Ability to sit on the ball correctly.

Procedure

Direct students to do the following:

1. Sit on the ball correctly.
2. Properly grasp resistance band.
3. Hold band shoulder-width apart, resting hands on knees.
4. Keep one hand on the knee and raise the other arm overhead, keeping elbow straight.
5. Slowly return to starting position.
6. Repeat five times.
7. Repeat sequence with other arm.

Key Points

- Maintain optimal posture.
- Tighten abdominal muscles.
- Inhale while stretching; exhale while relaxing.
- Keep band taut and wrists straight.

Variations

- Perform exercise with one foot raised off floor. Repeat with other foot.

Adaptations

- Use a physio-roll or underinflated ball.
- Only raise arm through partial range.
- Allow elbow to bend as arm raises.
- Use lighter resistance band or no band.
- Have paraeducator assist student, according to disability.

APENS (1995)

Standard 3.03: Emphasize strength-training programs for hypotonic individuals.

Standard 6.06: Provide activities that increase pressure on body surfaces, joints, and muscles, such as pushing and pulling.

SHOULDER ABDUCTION

Purpose

To strengthen shoulder abductor muscles and spine extensors using a resistance band.

Aspect

Strength.

NASPE Standards (1995)

Standard 4, benchmark for fourth grade: Engages in appropriate activity that results in the development of muscular strength.

Standard 4, benchmark for sixth grade: Correctly demonstrates activities designed to improve and maintain muscular strength and endurance, flexibility, cardiorespiratory functioning, and proper body composition.

Prerequisite Skills

Ability to sit on the ball correctly.

Procedure

Direct students to do the following:

1. Sit on the ball correctly.
2. Properly grasp resistance band shoulder-width apart.
3. Place band on knee of one leg.
4. Raise the outside arm out to the side and up as high as possible, keeping elbow straight and inside hand still.
5. Slowly return to starting position.
6. Repeat five times.
7. Repeat sequence with other arm.

Key Points

- Maintain optimal posture.
- Tighten abdominal muscles.
- Inhale while stretching; exhale while relaxing.
- Keep band taut and wrists straight.

Variations

- Perform exercise with one foot raised off floor. Repeat with other foot.

Adaptations

- Use a physio-roll or underinflated ball.
- Have paraeducator assist student, according to disability.
- Only raise arm through partial range.
- Allow elbow to bend as arm raises.
- Use lighter resistance band or no band.

APENS (1995)

Standard 3.03: Emphasize strength-training programs for hypotonic individuals.

Standard 6.06: Provide activities that increase pressure on body surfaces, joints, and muscles, such as pushing and pulling.

DOUBLE BICEPS CURL

Purpose
To strengthen biceps and spine extensors using a resistance band.

Aspect
Strength.

NASPE Standards (1995)
Standard 4, benchmark for fourth grade: Engages in appropriate activity that results in the development of muscular strength.

Standard 4, benchmark for sixth grade: Correctly demonstrates activities designed to improve and maintain muscular strength and endurance, flexibility, cardiorespiratory functioning, and proper body composition.

Prerequisite Skills
Ability to sit on the ball correctly.

Procedure
Direct students to do the following:
1. Sit on the ball correctly.
2. Properly grasp resistance band shoulder-width apart.
3. Place band under thighs of both legs.
4. With palms up, bend both elbows as far as possible.
5. Slowly return to starting position.
6. Repeat sequence five times.

Key Points
- Maintain optimal posture.
- Tighten abdominal muscles.
- Inhale while stretching; exhale while relaxing.
- Keep band taut and wrists straight.

Variations
- Perform exercise with one foot raised off floor. Repeat with other foot.

Adaptations
- Use a physio-roll or underinflated ball.
- Only bend elbows through partial range.
- Move one arm at a time.
- Use lighter resistance band or no band.
- Have paraeducator assist student, according to disability.

APENS (1995)
Standard 3.03: Emphasize strength-training programs for hypotonic individuals.

Standard 6.06: Provide activities that increase pressure on body surfaces, joints, and muscles, such as pushing and pulling.

CHOP AND LIFT

Purpose
To strengthen shoulder flexors and spine extensors using a resistance band.

Aspect
Strength.

NASPE Standards (1995)
Standard 4, benchmark for fourth grade: Engages in appropriate activity that results in the development of muscular strength.

Standard 4, benchmark for sixth grade: Correctly demonstrates activities designed to improve and maintain muscular strength and endurance, flexibility, cardiorespiratory functioning, and proper body composition.

Prerequisite Skills
Ability to sit on the ball correctly.

Procedure
Direct students to do the following:

1. Sit on the ball correctly.
2. Place one end of band under one foot and grasp band with both hands at waist level.
3. Raise straight arms on a diagonal above opposite shoulder.
4. Slowly return to starting position.
5. Repeat five times.
6. Repeat sequence to other side.

Key Points
- Maintain optimal posture.
- Tighten abdominal muscles.
- Inhale while stretching; exhale while relaxing.
- Keep band taut and wrists straight.

Variations
- Perform exercise with other foot raised off floor. Repeat with other foot.

Adaptations
- Use a physio-roll or underinflated ball.
- Only raise arms through partial range.
- Allow elbows to bend.
- Use lighter resistance band or no band.
- Have paraeducator assist student, according to disability.

APENS (1995)
Standard 3.03: Emphasize strength-training programs for hypotonic individuals.

Standard 6.06: Provide activities that increase pressure on body surfaces, joints, and muscles, such as pushing and pulling.

HIP ABDUCTION

Purpose

To strengthen hip abductors and spine extensors using a resistance band.

Aspect

Strength.

NASPE Standards (1995)

Standard 4, benchmark for fourth grade: Engages in appropriate activity that results in the development of muscular strength.

Standard 4, benchmark for sixth grade: Correctly demonstrates activities designed to improve and maintain muscular strength and endurance, flexibility, cardiorespiratory functioning, and proper body composition.

Prerequisite Skills

Ability to sit on the ball correctly.

Procedure

Direct students to do the following:

1. Sit on the ball correctly.
2. Place band around thighs immediately above knees.
3. Hold band together with both hands on one leg, forming a ring around thighs.
4. Step other leg out to the side as far as possible.
5. Slowly return to starting position.
6. Repeat five times.
7. Repeat sequence to other side.

Key Points

- Maintain optimal posture.
- Tighten abdominal muscles.
- Inhale while stretching; exhale while relaxing.
- Keep band taut and wrists straight.

Variations

- Perform exercise with heel of stationary foot raised off floor. Repeat with other side.

Adaptations

- Use a physio-roll or underinflated ball.
- Only move leg through partial range.
- Loosen ring of band.
- Use lighter resistance band or no band.
- Have paraeducator assist student, according to disability.

APENS (1995)

Standard 3.03: Emphasize strength-training programs for hypotonic individuals.

Standard 6.06: Provide activities that increase pressure on body surfaces, joints, and muscles, such as pushing and pulling.

LEG PRESS

Purpose

To strengthen hip and knee extensor muscles and spine extensors using a resistance band.

Aspect

Strength.

NASPE Standards (1995)

Standard 4, benchmark for fourth grade: Engages in appropriate activity that results in the development of muscular strength.

Standard 4, benchmark for sixth grade: Correctly demonstrates activities designed to improve and maintain muscular strength and endurance, flexibility, cardiorespiratory functioning, and proper body composition.

Prerequisite Skills

Ability to sit on the ball correctly.

Procedure

Direct students to do the following:

1. Sit on the ball correctly.
2. Grasp the ends of the band with both hands.
3. Lift one foot and bend knee to place the center of the band under arch of that foot.
4. Keep elbows still at sides of body and straighten out hip and knee.
5. Slowly return to starting position.
6. Repeat five times.
7. Repeat sequence with other side.

Key Points

- Maintain optimal posture.
- Tighten abdominal muscles.
- Inhale while stretching; exhale while relaxing.
- Keep band taught and wrists straight.

Variations

- Shorten length of band.

Adaptations

- Use a physio-roll or underinflated ball.
- Only move leg through partial range.
- Use lighter resistance band or no band.
- Have paraeducator assist student, according to disability.

APENS (1995)

Standard 3.03: Emphasize strength-training programs for hypotonic individuals.

Standard 6.06: Provide activities that increase pressure on body surfaces, joints, and muscles, such as pushing and pulling.

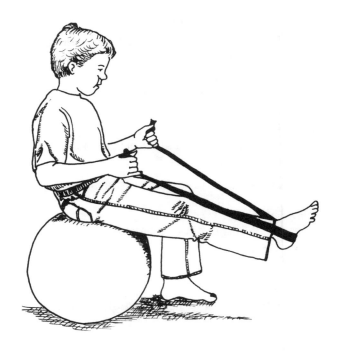

For cardiovascular fitness, you can use the ball like a chair in aerobics by having students perform all foot, leg, and arm move combinations while bouncing on the ball. Develop balance and trunk strength as well by using the ball for fitness training. Students will also tone their abdominals, backs, thighs, buttocks, and arms—all while improving the cardiovascular system.

Music

Use music that has a tempo of approximately 120 beats per minute (or slightly slower), which allows for the bounce and rebound of the ball. A faster tempo will be difficult to keep up with, tending to cause the students to lose balance as they move too quickly to stay with the beat.

9.22

CARDIOVASCULAR WARM-UP AND COOL-DOWN

Purpose
To warm up for or cool down after a cardiovascular workout.

Aspect
Fitness.

NASPE Standards (1995)
Standard 4, benchmark for fourth grade: Maintains continuous aerobic activity for a specific time or activity.

Prerequisite Skills
Ability to do balance and coordination activities on the ball.

Procedure
Direct students to move individual body parts without bouncing.

1. Shoulders—Raise and lower shoulders (shrugs), first right, then left, and then together.
2. Hips—Do the hip moves described in Activity 5.8.
3. Arms—Do the arm raises in Activity 5.9.
4. Feet—March in place and do toe and heel moves in Activities 5.10, 5.11, 5.12, and 5.13.

Key Points
- Use slower music for the warm-up.
- Explain to students that the warm-up prepares the body for the aerobic portion of the workout by doing similar moves at a slower pace.
- A cool-down helps the body to return slowly and safely to its nonexercise state.

Variations
- Add slow bouncing.
- Repeat the arm and foot moves while bouncing.

Adaptations
- Use a physio-roll or underinflated ball.
- Have paraeducator assist student, according to disability.

APENS (1995)
Standard 6.06: Adapt equipment.

Standard 10.04: Use paraprofessionals and peer tutors for individuals who require greater attention.

Use the rest of the activities in this chapter in the order presented to create a complete cardiovascular workout while bouncing on the ball. When first beginning on the ball, have students use arms and feet separately. Next, have them combine arm and foot moves. Use all the moves from the coordination chapter (chapter 6) to develop routines and any arm movements used in aerobic workouts (Biceps Curls, Triceps Press, Pectoral Press, Arm Punches, Upright Rows, Horizontal Arm Raises, and Power Pumps). Do each move for 16 counts, then move on to the next move. Use these activities as examples, then create your own!

9.23

CARDIOVASCULAR WORKOUT—ARMS

Purpose
To use arm moves while bouncing continuously on the Swiss Ball.

Aspect
Cardiovascular fitness.

NASPE Standards (1995)
Standard 4, benchmark for fourth grade: Maintains continuous aerobic activity for a specific time or activity.

Prerequisite Skills
Ability to do the coordination arm moves (see chapter 6).

Procedure
Direct students to sit on the ball and bounce while performing the following moves:

1. Bicep Curl: Hold arms in an "L," forearms parallel to thighs, palms up. Curl arms to shoulder and back down in two counts.

2. Tricep Press: Hold arms in curl position and slightly to sides of thighs. Press arms back and return to starting position in two counts.

3. Pectoral Press: Hold arms in an "L," elbows shoulder-high, hands higher than head. Press forearms together and pull apart in two counts.

4. Arm Raises Forward: Raise straight arms forward to shoulder level and down in two counts.

5. Horizontal Arm Raises: Raise straight arms sideways to shoulder level and down in two counts.

6. Power Pumps: Hold arms bent in a 90 degree angle with elbows at sides and fists forward. Pump arms back and forth as if power walking or running.

7. Upright Rows: Hold hands together at waist. Raise both hands to chin with elbows raising to shoulder height. Squeeze shoulder blades together.

Key Points
- Contract arm muscles during both phases of the movement.
- Make each movement strong and precise.

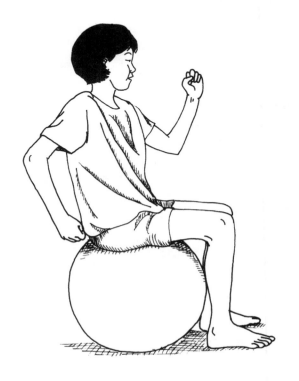

Variations

Use other moves from chapter 6:

- Arm Punches (Activity 6.11)
- Bow and Arrow Arms (variation of Activity 6.11)
- Jack Arms (variation of Activity 6.10)

Adaptations

- Use four counts for each movement.
- Do each arm movement for fewer repetitions.

- Use a physio-roll or underinflated ball.
- Have paraeducator assist student, according to disability.

APENS (1995)

Standard 10.04: Identify and create goal levels for each skill or activity that will allow all individuals with disabilities to achieve levels of success at the same time.

9.24

CARDIOVASCULAR WORKOUT—FEET

Purpose

To use foot moves while bouncing continuously on the ball.

Aspect

Cardiovascular fitness.

NASPE Standards (1995)

Standard 4, benchmark for fourth grade: Maintains continuous aerobic activity for a specific time or activity.

Prerequisite Skills

Ability to do foot moves on the ball (see chapter 6).

Procedure

Use foot moves from chapter 5, such as side toe touch and variations (Activity 5.12) and side straddle and variations (Activity 5.14) linking them one after another.

Key Points

- Select moves that exercise a variety of leg muscles.
- Alternate single-foot moves with jumps for a steady workout.

Variations

- Use only single-foot moves for a lower intensity workout and only jumps for a higher intensity workout.

Adaptations

- Do foot moves in four or more counts.

- Use fewer repetitions if aerobic capacity is an issue.
- Use a physio-roll or underinflated ball.
- Have paraeducator assist student, according to disability.

APENS (1995)

Standard 10.04: Identify and create goal levels for each skill or activity that will allow all individuals with disabilities to achieve levels of success at the same time.

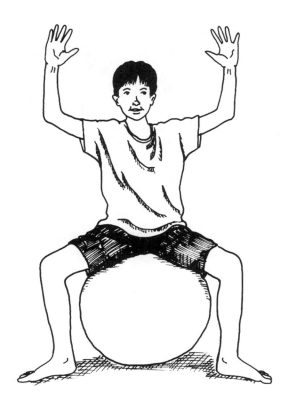

CHAPTER 10

MANIPULATIVE AND GYMNASTIC SKILLS

In this chapter, we'll explain how Swiss Balls are used in manipulative activities. Using the balls as manipulatives creates immediate excitement for students of all ages, because they are delighted with the quick success they experience performing manipulative skills. How does the Swiss Ball help? The increased size and weight of the Swiss Ball give students more feedback. Feedback, in turn, allows students to feel the alignment and position of their body parts as they manipulate the ball in a variety of ways. As an extension of these concepts, we'll outline how you can incorporate the Swiss Ball into gymnastics.

Manipulative Skills

All students need to learn how to handle equipment skillfully to help them master activities of daily living. Using the Swiss Balls to help teach manipulative skills has especially helped children with vision and processing problems. Through size and color alone, the balls excite and motivate all students who are drawn like magnets to explore the balls. Students see rolling, tossing, catching, volleying, and dribbling in a new light when using the Swiss Balls. For your planning convenience, we have organized the activities in this section from least to most difficult.

ROLLING

Purpose
To develop rolling skills.

Aspect
Rolling.

NASPE Standards (1995)
Standard 2, benchmark for kindergarten: Identifies the fundamental manipulative pattern of rolling an object.

Standard 5, benchmark for kindergarten: Takes turns using a piece of equipment.

Procedure
Direct students to do the following:

1. Travel, rolling the ball from point A to point B.
2. Return.

Key Points
- Keep the ball on floor.
- Stand behind the ball and push with hands.

Variations
- Travel, rolling the ball at different speeds and with varying force.
- Travel, rolling the ball with one or two other people.
- Roll the ball to a partner:
  - Begin seated on floor with the ball between the legs.
  - Roll while standing.
  - Most challenging, roll the ball backward between legs.

Adaptations
- Use physio-roll or underinflated ball.
- Have paraeducator assist student, according to disability.

APENS (1995)
Standard 6.06: Adapt equipment.

Standard 10.01: Use group activities to promote cooperative learning development.

The next two skills, the Lift and Carry, are the two most basic manipulative skills for protecting the spine. If students learn the correct mechanics at a young age, they have a good chance of developing good lifelong habits for a healthy, pain-free back. Use these two as well as more advanced carries to get started.

10.2

LIFT

Purpose
To teach proper lifting techniques to protect the spine.

Aspect
Lifting.

NASPE Standards (1995)
Standard 2, benchmark for kindergarten: Identifies and begins to utilize the technique employed for lifting.

Prerequisite Skills
None.

Procedure
Direct students to do the following:

1. Place the ball on a floor marker.
2. Place feet in forward stance with front foot close to the side of the ball.
3. Keeping back straight, lean forward at hips, and bend knees, keeping knees over feet.
4. Focusing eyes on ball, grasp ball and pull it into body, pushing buttocks back. Do not allow spine to curve.
5. Straighten knees to lift ball to medium level.
6. Replace the ball on floor marker, using proper lowering technique. Bend knees and keep back straight as the ball is lowered to the floor.

Key Points
- Keep feet apart.
- Lift with hip and leg muscles, not back muscles.
- Keep spine in proper alignment.
- Keep the ball close to body.
- Avoid twisting or bending the spine while lifting.

Variations
- Lifting to Different Levels: Lift the ball to high level, then lower it to low level.
- Lifting With Other Body Parts: Lie on back and lift the ball from floor with feet. Then transfer the ball to hands.

Adaptations

- Use underinflated or smaller ball.
- Have paraeducator assist student, according to disability.

APENS (1995)

Standard 2.01: Structure tasks and activities to stimulate and facilitate normal postural response.

Standard 10.02: Teach the correct form necessary to perform the skill.

10.3

CARRY

Purpose

To carry the Swiss Ball safely and correctly.

Aspect

Carrying.

NASPE Standards (1995)

Standard 2, benchmark for kindergarten: Identifies and uses a variety of relationships with objects (e.g., over and under, behind, alongside, through).

Prerequisite Skills

Ability to lift the Swiss Ball safely and correctly.

Procedure

Direct students to do the following:

1. Carry a ball from storage area (behind a bench or tumbling mat, inside hoops, or the like) to a floor marker.
2. Discuss, demonstrate, and practice the different ways students carried the ball: in front of the body, on the side of the body, overhead.
3. Carry the ball from point A to point B.

Key Points

- Keep the body aligned in optimal posture.

Variations

- Carry the ball along different pathways.
- Carry the ball while traveling in forward, backward, or sideways directions.
- Do the Crab Walk with the ball on stomach.

Adaptations

- Use underinflated or smaller ball.
- Have paraeducator assist student, according to disability.

APENS (1995)

Standard 6.06: Use floor spots for "home base." Use different size and weight balls.

BELLY BUSTERS

Purpose

To move the Swiss Ball with a partner for a cooperative challenge.

Aspect

Cooperation.

NASPE Standards (1995)

Standard 7, benchmark for kindergarten: Experiences positive feelings as a result of involvement in physical activity.

Standard 7, benchmark for kindergarten: Celebrates personal successes and achievements as well as those of others.

Prerequisite Skills

Ability to lift and carry correctly.

Procedure

Direct students to do the following:

1. Stand facing a partner.
2. Place and hold the Swiss Ball between partners' "bellies."
3. Move from point A to point B, keeping the ball between them.

Key Points

- Progress from a stationary position to dynamic movement (travelling).
- Begin with both hands holding the ball, next one hand, then no hands.

Variations

- Wacky Backs: Have (or help) students put the ball between their backs and then try to travel.
- Side Sticker: Have (or help) students put the ball between their sides. Extending inside arm overhead is helpful. Try opposite side. Have one student facing forward, the other, backward.

- Rotating Robots: Start with Belly Busters, then both partners turn to right or left at the same time, keeping the ball trapped between them as they turn 180 degrees.

Adaptations

- Perform activity in stationary position only.
- Paraeducator assists students according to disability.

APENS (1995)

Standard 10.01: Design activities that allow individuals to work together in pairs.

Standard 10.01: Guides students to be peer tutors or partners to teach individuals with disabilities.

Tossing and catching seem simple and basic to students who have had experience with these skills, but in today's busy world not all parents have time to play catch with their children. Thus, many students are starting school with little, if any, experience with tossing and catching. The large size and bright color of the Swiss Ball make it easy for students to be successful tossing and catching, leading to greater success with smaller balls.

10.5

CATCH

Purpose
To catch the Swiss Ball with hands correctly.

Aspect
Catching, receiving.

NASPE Standards (1995)
Standard 1, benchmark for kindergarten: Identifies and begins to utilize the technique employed to catch an object.

Prerequisite Skills
Ability to roll the Swiss Ball correctly.

Procedure
1. Have students work in partners or 3s.
2. Roll the ball to your partner, who, in turn, catches the ball with hands.
3. Have receiving student roll the ball back to partner and continue practice around the circle.

Key Points
- Keep eyes on the ball.
- Stop the ball with hands only.

Variations
- Have students roll the ball while standing.
- Add activities such as Drop and Stop, Bounce and Catch With a Partner, Bounce and Catch Against a Wall, Toss and Catch With a Partner.
- Trap ball with body and hands.

Adaptations
- Use underinflated ball or physio-roll.
- Have paraeducator assist student, according to disability.

APENS (1995)
Standard 6.06: Use simple to complex skills. Create activities that encourage peer interaction in a small group.

DROP AND CATCH

Purpose

To teach the skills of tossing and catching using the Swiss Balls to develop hand-to-eye coordination.

Aspect

Tossing and catching.

NASPE Standards (1995)

Standard 1, benchmark for kindergarten: Tosses a ball and catches it before it bounces twice.

Procedure

Direct students to do the following:

1. Begin in a self-space with a ball.
2. Watch teacher demonstrate a Drop and Catch from waist level.
3. Have students hold the ball at waist level and try it.
4. Practice.

Key Points

- Keep feet apart with one foot slightly ahead of the other.
- Bend knees.
- Keep eyes on the ball.
- Bring the ball in toward body as it is caught.
- The size of the ball will help most students achieve immediate success.

Variations

- Try Toss and Catch and Drop and Catch combinations.
- Add a clap before catching the ball.
- Add a turn before catching the ball.
- Touch ground before catching the ball.

Adaptations

- Have paraeducator assist student, according to disability.
- Assist by standing beside or behind the student and guiding their hands.
- Give physical support as student first attempts the Drop and Catch.
- Trade the Swiss Ball for a ball of different size and weight: beach ball, slo-mo ball, or medicine ball.

APENS (1995)

Standard 2.01: Select and design activities to stimulate the development of intersensory and intrasensory integration.

HAND DRIBBLE

Purpose
To keep the Swiss Ball in motion using hands as an easy introduction to dribbling.

Aspect
Dribbling with hands.

NASPE Standards (1995)
Standard 1, benchmark for sixth grade: Hand dribbles while preventing an opponent from stealing the ball.

Standard 2, benchmark for kindergarten: Establishes a beginning movement vocabulary (personal space, high and low levels, light and strong force).

Standard 2, benchmark for second grade: Receives and sends an object in a continuous motion.

Procedure
Direct students to do the following:

1. Assume the ready position: feet shoulder-width apart with knees bent and one foot slightly in front of the other.
2. Start dribbling with fingers spread apart and curved, pushing down gently so the ball returns to waist level.
3. Keep the ball moving up and down in a continuous motion.

Key Points
- Be sure to assume the ready position.
- Keep fingers spread.
- Bounce to waist level.
- Stay in self-space.

Variations
- Move through general space about the room without touching anyone.
- Advanced dribblers can play Dribble Tag: Give everyone a ball. Designate taggers. Explain that the object is to stay away from the taggers. If touched by a tagger, stop and hold the ball at waist level. Other students tap the tagged person to free them so they can return to the game.

- Basketball Tag: Same as Dribble Tag except everyone being chased is dribbling a basketball and the taggers each use a Swiss Ball.

Adaptations
- Trade the Swiss Ball for a ball of different size and weight, such as a beach ball, volleyball, or basketball.
- Have paraeducator assist student, according to disability.
- Allow additional practice time.
- Carry the ball while others dribble.
- Take students in wheelchairs out of the chair to an alternative safe place where they can practice.

APENS (1995)
Standard 10.01: Select tasks that can be performed by the individual with a disability individually and safely.

Standard 6.06: Allow for appropriate additional practice.

SUPINE KICK

Purpose
To practice kicking using the correct muscles and part of the foot.

Aspect
Kicking.

NASPE Standards (1995)
Standard 1, benchmark for second grade: Kicks from supine position with accuracy to a partner.

Procedure
Direct students to do the following:

1. First student lies on his or her back with legs up in a frog-style position.
2. Teacher or the second student gently tosses the ball underhand toward the first student's feet.
3. Kicker flexes his or her knees and kicks the ball back to tosser.

Key Points
- Kicker lies on back with legs in air.
- Tosser should aim just above feet, throwing underhand.
- Kicker kicks gently, aiming at tosser.

Variations
- Stand up and gently kick the ball to a partner.
- Move into general space kicking the ball back and forth with a partner.

Adaptations
- Have paraeducator assist student, according to disability.
- Use lighter or smaller balls (e.g., a 35-centimeter ball) or both.

APENS (1995)
Standard 3.01: Utilize nonweight-bearing activities or simplified weight-bearing activities.

KICKING

Purpose
To kick correctly under control and to provide extra feedback to the body from the extra weight of the ball to improve mechanics.

Aspect
Kicking.

NASPE Standards (1995)
Standard 1, benchmark for kindergarten: Kicks a ball using a smooth continuous running step.

Procedure
Direct students to do the following:
1. Place Swiss Balls on floor spots.
2. Kick a stationary Swiss Ball from a stationary position to wall.
3. Return the Swiss Ball to the floor marker before each kick.

Key Points
- Ensure the non-kicking foot is placed to side of the ball.
- Contact the ball with the instep of the kicking foot behind the center of the ball.

Variations
- Run to kick a stationary ball.
- Kick a ball rolled by a teacher or skilled student.
- Progress to tapping and dribbling a Swiss Ball while moving.

Adaptations
- Have paraeducator assist student, according to disability.
- Allow additional practice time.
- Use a smaller ball.

APENS (1995)
Standard 6.06: Use simple to complex skills. Use floor spots for "home base."

FOOT DRIBBLE

Purpose

To keep the Swiss Ball in motion using the feet as an introduction or alternative to standard balls.

Aspect

Dribbling with the feet.

NASPE Standards (1995)

Standard 1, benchmark for second grade: Foot dribbles the Swiss Ball with control.

Prerequisite Skills

Ability to kick a ball, standing and supine.

Procedure

Direct students to do the following:

1. Have students sit in self-space.
2. Touch the inside, outside, and instep of both feet. These are the parts of the feet that will keep the ball in motion.
3. Have students get a ball and practice tapping it with the different parts of the feet, keeping it in their self-space.
4. Ensure the ball stays in contact with floor.

Key Points

- Keep the ball very close to the feet after each touch.
- Use both feet, but not in strict alternation.

Variations

- Foot dribble in general space.
- Dribble around cones.
- Dribble Tag: Explain that the object is to stay away from the taggers. If touched by a tagger, stop and trap the ball with the feet. Other students tap the tagged person to free them so they can return to the game.

Adaptations

- Have paraeducator assist student, according to disability.
- Allow additional practice time.
- Students in wheelchairs can carry an appropriately sized ball or squeeze a smaller ball between feet or knees.
- Use a smaller ball.

APENS (1995)

Standard 6.06: Provide for extra practice. Adapt equipment.

VOLLEY WITH A BOUNCE

Purpose

To provide kinesthetic feedback and aid understanding of the mechanics of continuous motion.

Aspect

Volleying.

NASPE Standards (1995)

Standard 1, benchmark for second grade: Receives and sends an object in a continuous motion.

Prerequisite Skills

Ability to toss and catch a Swiss Ball.

Procedure

Direct students to do the following:

1. Assume the ready position: feet shoulder-width apart, knees bent, and one foot slightly in front of the other.

2. Use hands to direct a ball using an underhand motion toward a person or a wall without catching or holding the ball.

Key Points

- Emphasize correct ready position.

Adaptations

- Use a gentle toss and catch.
- Guide student's hands through the motion.

APENS (1995)

Standard 6.06: Use different size and weight balls. Use simple to complex skills. Provide for extra practice.

TOSSING AND CATCHING WHILE SEATED ON THE BALL

Purpose

To develop the coordination to toss and catch other balls while sitting correctly on a Swiss Ball.

Aspect

Tossing and catching balls.

NASPE Standards (1995)

Standard 1, benchmark for fourth grade: Tosses and catches a variety of balls; balances with control on a variety of objects.

Prerequisite Skills

Ability to sit on the ball correctly and toss and catch a variety of balls while standing.

Procedure

Direct students to do the following:

1. Form circles from five to eight feet in diameter with three to six members, each sitting on a ball.
2. Sit on ball correctly.
3. Toss smaller balls (e.g., Koosh, yarn, Nerf, beach, and small medicine) to each other.
4. Thrower calls catcher's name, then catcher replies, "Ready!" before thrower may throw small ball.

Key Points

- Ensure thrower waits for catcher to state he or she is ready.
- Use proper mechanics for underhand toss.
- Use correct catching technique.
- Check for correct sitting position.

Variations

- Throw small balls of varying textures, sizes, and weights.

Adaptations

- Place in smaller groups of three or four.
- Have paraeducator assist student, according to disability.

APENS (1995)

Standard 5.09: Utilize philosophy that supports cooperation. Advocate for a variety of support in the regular physical education setting.

Gymnastics

The Swiss Ball makes a wonderful gymnastics prop. Not only can students use it for extensive stretching and strengthening activities (see chapters 8 and 9), they can also use it for support and in partner and individual routines. For example, have students use the ball as a headstand helper against a wall to support back but not legs. Have students hug the ball to do log rolls and shoulder rolls, and in the case of a shoulder roll, students can lift the ball to stand. In addition, students can use the ball to create rhythmic gymnastics routines either alone or with a partner. Advanced students may want to add them to floor routines, depending on ability. Note, however, that while using the balls to work on gymnastics activities, you must use mats for safety.

10.13

GYMNASTICS

Purpose

To practice gymnastics skills with the support of the Swiss Ball.

Aspect

Traveling, rotation, and balance.

NASPE Standards (1995)

Standard 2, benchmark for fourth grade: Transfers weight from feet to hands at fast and slow speeds using large extensions (e.g., Mule Kick, Handstand Cartwheel, Back Limber, Back Walk-Out.)

Prerequisite Skills

Ability to balance, transfer weight, roll, fall and land, and do prone rocking and roll.

Procedure

Review Prone Rocking (Activity 5.18, Side to Side variation). Then direct students to do the following:

1. Begin at one end of tumbling mat and roll sideways the length of mat.
2. Begin on top of the ball, roll off one side, and continue rolling until back up on top of the ball, doing several in a sequence.

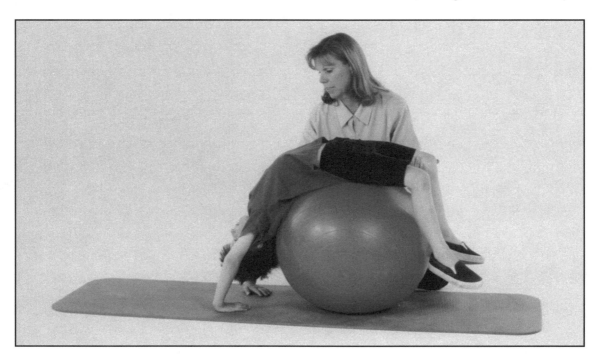

Key Points

- Move body slowly, smoothly, and with control.
- Bend at joints to absorb force of weight transfer.

Variations

- The Swiss Ball helps support the Back Limber:
  1. Begin in a supine position on the ball, feet on mat.
  2. Arch body over the ball, stretching arms overhead until hands touch mat.
  3. Have eyes follow hands while back of head rests on the ball.
  4. Lift both legs over the head and allow them to land on mat together on opposite side of the ball. (Be sure to have a spotter hold the ball still during this activity.)
- Mule kick with the stomach on the ball, hands resting in front of the ball, and kick up legs.

- Handstands can be spotted with the ball against the wall so the ball supports the back.
- Cartwheels can be performed over the ball as you would use a tumbling aid to reach over.
- Back Walk Outs can also be done over the ball when the ball is held by two students or a teacher and a student. Advanced gymnasts can do this move without the spotters if the ball is still.

Adaptations

- Have paraeducator assist student, according to disability.
- Use underinflated ball or physio-roll.

APENS (1995)

Standard 6.06: Use simple to complex skills. Use floor spots for "home base." Provide activities that increase pressure on body surfaces, joints, and muscles, such as pushing and pulling.

CHAPTER 11

GAMES

The Swiss Balls add a whole new dimension to games. Whether students are standing up, lying on the floor, or sitting on the ball, you will find the games in this chapter can lead students into both sports and life skills. Students socialize and cooperate better, too; because they are absorbed in the challenge of moving on and with the ball, all the extraneous social issues seem to vanish. In this chapter, we will share many ideas for games generated both by students and teachers. Then, we'll focus on specific cooperative learning activities. Finally, we will include a lesson plan for combining Swiss Balls with a Jump Rope for Heart event.

Games

Games help children learn to interact while developing physical skills. In short, they're practice, but they're fun. So introduce the balls to increase communication between students and refine physical skills that will carry over to balls of different sizes and shapes.

FOLLOW THE LEADER

Purpose

To encourage group cooperation and self-expression.

Aspect

Balance, coordination, leadership.

NASPE Standards (1995)

Standard 5, benchmark for second grade: Uses equipment and space safely and properly.

Standard 6, benchmark for second grade: Appreciates the benefits that accompany cooperation and sharing.

Prerequisite Skills

Know rules of Follow the Leader, ability to do balance and coordination activities (see chapters 5 and 6).

Procedure

Set up and play the game as follows:

1. Sit on the ball correctly in self-space, in circle formation.
2. Watch teacher demonstrate a familiar skill while seated.
3. Try same skill while remaining in self-space.
4. One student volunteers to be the next "leader," then performs the skill while seated and all others follow the leader.
5. Continue until all students have had a chance to share.

Key Points

- Use sit-down activities.
- Remain in self-space.
- Encourage everyone to follow the leader.
- Each new leader should choose a different skill.
- Give everyone the option of leading or not (the teacher should encourage all students to try leading at least once).

Variations

- Balance in supine or prone positions.
- Body Rhythms: Keep the beat of a drum or music while performing coordination skill.
- Add the chant, "Everybody follow me;

everybody follow, follow, follow; everybody follow, follow me (or insert the name of a student)." Next, demonstrate a skill for students to follow. Then, insert a student's name into chant. Continue until all have had a chance to lead.

Adaptations

- Use a physio-roll or underinflated ball.
- Use floor spots to mark self-space.
- Decrease the size of the circle or the number of students in each circle or both.

- Lie on floor and move ball with hands or feet.
- Have paraeducator assist student, according to disability.

APENS (1995)

Standard 6.06: Use floor spots for "home base."

Standard 10.02: Play cooperative games which foster social interactions and trust for individuals with and without disabilities.

11.2

CIRCLE BALL

Purpose

To encourage group cooperation.

Aspect

Passing, receiving, stopping on signal.

NASPE Standards (1995)

Standard 5, benchmark for second grade: Stops activity immediately upon the signal to do so.

Procedure

Set up and play the game as follows:

1. Stand and form circles of six to eight students.

2. Pass the ball, using hands, to the person next to them.

3. Continue passing around the circle in one direction until the stop signal is given.

Key Points

- Keep the ball moving smoothly around the circle.
- Be ready to receive the ball.
- Pass the ball as soon as possible.
- Stop on signal.

Variations

- Face the outside of the circle.
- Form a straight line and pass the ball overhead. The last in line brings the ball to the front so passing can begin again.
- Pass the ball at a faster or slower speed.
- Add a beat and pass the ball to the beat.
- Pass the ball at a low, medium, or high level.
- Make the circle bigger and take the necessary amount of steps to pass and receive the ball successfully.

Adaptations

- Decrease size of circle or number of students in each circle or both.
- Sit on floor to pass ball.
- Use a smaller or underinflated ball.
- Have paraeducator assist student, according to disability.

APENS (1995)

Standard 6.06: Create activities that encourage peer interaction in a small group basis. Use different size and weight balls.

11.3

HOT POTATO GAME

Purpose

To practice throwing and catching the Swiss Ball in a game-like setting.

Aspect

Tossing and catching.

NASPE Standards (1995)

Standard 1, benchmark for sixth grade: Throws a variety of objects, demonstrating both accuracy and force.

Prerequisite Skills

Ability to toss and catch any ball.

Procedure

Set up and play the game as follows:

1. Stand in a circle, five to eight feet in diameter. There should be four to five students per circle.
2. Start by simply throwing gently to anyone in the circle and catching the Swiss Ball.
3. Call out the name of the student who is expected to catch the ball.

Key Points

- Stay in the ready position: arms and hands out and away from the body ready to catch the ball.
- Keep eyes on the ball at all times.
- Be sure to emphasize communication. Call a person's name and make eye contact before throwing.

Variations

- Add music.
- Form several groups of three to five people. Have students pass the ball around the circle with the music. Stop the music and have the person holding the ball rotate clockwise to the next closest group so that all groups lose and gain a player each time the music stops.

Adaptations

- Start by sitting on the floor or in a chair.
- Give verbal cues and reminders.
- Use a smaller or underinflated ball.
- Have paraeducator assist student, according to disability.

APENS (1995)

Standard 6.06: Reinforce auditory directions with visual cues. Create activities that encourage peer interaction in a small group basis.

ROLL YOUR WAY TO FITNESS

Purpose

To develop fitness through six different learning centers.

Aspect

Strength, flexibility, and aerobic capacity.

NASPE Standard (1995)

Standard 4, benchmarks for fourth grade: Engages in appropriate activity that results in the development of muscular strength. Maintains continuous aerobic activity for a specific time or activity. Supports, lifts, and controls body weight in a variety of activities. Regularly participates in physical activity for the purpose of improving physical fitness.

Prerequisite Skills

Ability to perform a wide variety of aerobic, strength, and flexibility exercises on the Swiss Balls independently.

Procedure

1. Hang the posters of the exercises from this book on all four walls of the gym. Place about 5 on each end wall and 10 on each of the two longer walls. Group strength, flexibility, and aerobic exercises together.

2. Use cones to mark six different locations for exercises (five posters each).

3. Clearly number each section, 1 through 6.

4. Place several large or small dice in the center of the room. (Use a carpet square for each small die to define a good tossing surface.)

5. Have students work alone or with a partner.

6. Each student carries a ball that is the correct size to the dice area and rolls one die to decide which of the six areas to go to.

7. Tell students the number of different exercises to perform and the times you want them repeated (e.g., choose four stretches from the flexibility center and four aerobic exercises to be performed 10 times each).

Key Points

- Ensure all balls are appropriately sized.
- Be sure all the exercises are familiar to the students.
- Have enough dice to get everyone started. (After they get started, their activity will be staggered.)
- With large classes if one station gets too crowded, the student should roll again or choose an area he or she has not yet visited.

Variations

- Also place dice in front of the aerobic and strength areas and have students roll to see how many times to perform each exercise.

Adaptations

- Have paraeducator assist student, according to disability, and provide adapted equipment as appropriate.

APENS (1995)

Standard 3.03: Emphasize strength-training programs. Emphasize flexibility exercise for individuals.

Standard 6.01: Adapt fitness activities to individuals with low motor skills.

As you probably well know, students usually have an immediate desire to talk and socialize with others in class. Indeed, the simple act of bouncing on the ball puts people in a good mood, making them want to talk. Although you should take your particular student population into careful consideration, the following social game activities are generally appropriate for fourth grade and up.

11.5

GETTING TO KNOW YOU

Purpose

To learn other students' names and interact socially while developing physical skills.

Aspect

Communication among students and spatial awareness.

NASPE Standard (1995)

Standard 7, benchmark for fourth grade: Experiences positive feelings as a result of involvement in physical activity. Celebrates personal successes and achievements as well as those of others.

Prerequisite Skills

Ability to sit correctly on the ball, spatial awareness, and coordination.

Procedure

Set up and play the game as follows:

1. Form groups of three to six and stand about one arm's-length apart in circles, five to eight feet in diameter.
2. Use floor markers to mark self-space. (Use bicycle tires or hula hoops if the balls roll.)
3. Sit on the ball correctly and begin to bounce gently.
4. Have each student say his or her name, one at a time.
5. One student begins by calling out own name and one other. The two people stand up and trade places.
6. Continue till everyone has had at least a couple turns.

Key Points

- Remind students to sit on the ball correctly.
- Be sure all students are one arm's-length away from each other in the circle.
- Remind students to stay in self-space as they move to other balls.
- Students may end up on a ball that is not the proper size, but this is OK for this activity.

Variations

- Practice trading places with a partner before working in a small group.
- As the game progresses, students can call more than two names at a time.
- Call "Scramble!"—everyone switches places.

Adaptations

- Use a physio-roll or underinflated ball.
- Reassign groups if someone is really struggling.
- Join the group that needs the most guidance.
- Adjust student's sitting position from the front.
- Give support from behind, if necessary.
- Have paraeducator assist student, according to disability, and provide adapted equipment as appropriate.

APENS (1995)

Standard 2.01: Structure tasks and activities to stimulate and facilitate normal postural responses. Develop and implement programs that stimulate vestibular, visual, and proprioceptive senses. Implement activities that stimulate upright postures and control of head, neck, and trunk.

11.6

BRAIN GAMES

Purpose

To integrate classroom studies (e.g., nutrition, health, and geography) while using Swiss Balls for students who need repetition with movement to remember facts.

Aspect

Memory, spatial awareness, and motor planning.

NASPE Standard (1995)

Standard 7, benchmarks for fourth grade: Experiences positive feelings as a result

of involvement in physical activity. Celebrates personal successes and achievements as well as those of others.

Prerequisite Skills

Ability to play the Getting to Know You game (Activity 11.5).

Procedure

Set up and play the game as follows:

1. Using the Getting to Know You game format, choose a subject from classroom studies.

2. Have each student name an item related to the designated topic (e.g., bones, muscles, fruits and vegetables, cities or countries). Repeat the choices until everyone can name them.

3. Have a student leader call out an item chosen by another student. These two students change places.

4. Continue until each student has had two or more turns.

Key Points

- Place color pictures of the chosen topic (e.g., Food Guide Pyramid, labeled muscle posters, or the like) in clear view.
- Use hoops or bicycle tires to hold balls in place.
- Emphasize using eyes and ears to help students focus.

Variations

- Change topics to fit any area of study.

Adaptations

- Use a physio-roll or underinflated ball.
- Have paraeducator assist students with remembering items and moving across the circle.

APENS (1995)

Standard 6.06: Reinforce auditory directions with visual cues. Create activities that encourage peer interaction in a small group.

Cooperative Learning Activities

While using the balls for cooperative activities, we have been amazed to see students eagerly holding hands and encouraging each other both physically and emotionally. We started using the pictures from Kucera's *Gymnastik mit dem Hüpfball* (1993) to encourage cooperation. We divided students into pairs or small groups and instructed them to try the activities depicted.

Note: We have found certain safety precautions effective. While students are attempting to recreate the activities in the pictures, they must have spotters who keep their feet on the floor and otherwise remain stable to physically support the partner or group members. For larger students, or special needs students, use two spotters. Monitor the students to make sure the spotters are performing appropriately and are numerous enough to support other group members and that different people take turns spotting. You may need to help spot for some larger students.

SEATED COOPERATIVE GAMES

Purpose

To teach students to encourage and support each other, both physically and emotionally.

Aspect

Balance and strength.

NASPE Standard (1995)

Standard 7, benchmark for fourth grade: Experiences positive feelings as a result of involvement in physical activity. Celebrates personal successes and achievements as well as those of others.

Prerequisite Skills

Ability to sit on the ball correctly, success in a variety of balancing positions on the Swiss Ball, and experience and success working cooperatively with others.

Procedure

Set up and play the game as follows:

1. Look at the "Sitting on the Ball Correctly" poster.

2. Create either pairs or groups of three.

3. Designate at least one spotter for each group. Have the spotter keep both feet flat on the floor and offer a strong supportive hand to those trying out the balance challenges.

4. Have one student in each group sit cross-legged on the ball. Strong and confident groups of three can have two people in the group sit cross-legged on top of the ball.

Key Points

- Ensure spotter keeps his or her feet on the floor and remains in a stable position to physically support partner or group members.

- Have two students spot larger students.

- Ensure all students take a turn spotting.

- Assist in spotting where needed.

Variations

- Lift one straight leg onto another group member's ball.

- If ready, encourage students to try lifting one leg, then both legs, off the floor.

- Use bent or straight legs.

Adaptations

- Place ball against a wall for added stability.

- Provide spotting assistance.

- Use underinflated ball.

- Have paraeducator assist students with remembering items and moving across the circle.

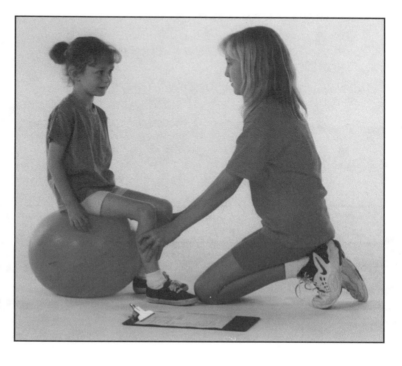

COOPERATIVE AIRPLANE

Purpose
To teach students to encourage and support each other, both physically and emotionally.

Aspect
Balance and strength.

NASPE Standard (1995)
Standard 7, benchmark for fourth grade: Experiences positive feelings as a result of involvement in physical activity. Celebrates personal successes and achievements as well as those of others.

Prerequisite Skills
Ability to do the Airplane (variation of Activity 5.12).

Procedure
Set up and play the game as follows:

1. Form a triangle about three feet across with three students.
2. Have all students lie prone with the stomach on the ball and join together by holding forearms.
3. Have one stabilizing student keep feet on the floor while the others lift off to the Airplane position.
4. Rotate stabilizing job within each group.

Key Points
- Practice Cooperative Airplane position until strong, balanced, and confident.
- Use two stabilizers per student where needed.
- Tell students to let go arms if anyone starts to lose balance.
- Caution: Be sure students can get hands free to put on floor to protect head.

Adaptations
- Use two stabilizers and only one person lifting off.
- Use a physio-roll or underinflated ball.
- Have paraeducator assist students if necessary.

APENS (1995)
Standard 5.10: Utilize philosophy that supports cooperation. Advocate for a variety of support in the regular physical education setting.

STANDING GROUP CHALLENGE

Purpose
To encourage group cooperation.

Aspect
Passing the Swiss Ball using the feet.

NASPE Standard (1995)
Standard 7, benchmark for fourth grade: Experiences positive feelings as a result of involvement in physical activity. Celebrates personal successes and achievements as well as those of others.

Prerequisite Skills

Ability to pass the Swiss Ball using the feet to a partner.

Procedure

Set up and play the game as follows:

1. Have groups of three to five students (each student with a ball) stand in circles, five to eight feet in diameter.
2. Have each student begin in the ready position: one foot on the floor and one foot resting on top of the Swiss Ball.
3. Designate a student to give the "Switch" signal upon which all students gently roll their balls with one foot to the right.
4. Direct students to stop the ball coming toward them and return to the ready position.

Key Points

- Remind students to return to the ready position each time they receive a ball.
- Have students take turns giving the signal when the whole group is ready.
- Use balance and control.

Variations

- Work only with a partner.
- For a slightly easier activity, have students bend over the ball

with both hands resting on the floor to create a tunnel for the ball to pass through. Be sure legs are hip-width apart and arms are shoulder-width apart. Upon the signal, all students pass the ball to the right, through the next tunnel.

Adaptations

- Allow students to use their hands.
- Have paraeducator assist student, according to disability.

APENS (1995)

Standard 6.01: Establish appropriate expectations and goals. Adapt fitness activities to individuals with low motor skills.

Jump Rope for Heart Integration

When Anne moved to her current teaching assignment at Rocky Mountain Elementary School in 1995, she had to adapt her teaching in many ways. Her new school is a "mega-center" school with a diverse population of special needs students, including those with multiple physical handicaps. One big change was the way she ran her Jump Rope for Heart event. We are including here an adaptation of the explanation she sent to her school site team coordinator for her new way of running her Jump Rope for Heart program to include all students during her normally scheduled school day.

ANNE'S ALTERNATIVE JUMP ROPE FOR HEART
Jump and Bounce for the Health of It

The two major reasons for trying a new approach to my Jump Rope for Heart were to be sure my diverse population of special needs students would be actively engaged and to add a dynamic but low-impact alternative to complement the rope jumping. All students were on task the entire time. The children spent the rest breaks on the balls stretching, strength training, and bouncing to continue the cardiovascular workout.

Since it was my first time through the alternative jump, I changed, modified, and moved things around as we went along. Here, I'll outline how to duplicate our smoothest jump—I mean bounce!—of the day.

Time: 50 minutes

Number of students: 50 to 65 per double class

Space: Large gym with steps that open to a stage area

Teachers and support services: physical educator, music, and paraeducators (for wheelchair and REACH students)

Warm-Up

1. Give each student a jump rope. (We used the special needs population pamphlet provided by the American Heart Association as needed. It was a great resource.)

2. Play music with a good beat while students jump rope to warm up.

3. Next, call out students' favorite rope-jumping tricks, allowing students to perform the ones they feel comfortable with.

4. When students start to look tired, stop and return the short ropes to various locations around the gym.

Setup

Before starting: Meet to demonstrate and discuss all the different centers available. The following are the ones we used:

Jump rope learning centers

Partner posters

Double Dutch

Trestle Tree with four long ropes

Posters with individual tricks

Video demonstrating tricks

Swiss Ball learning centers

Posters with line drawings and exercise explanations

Fit Ball video (see appendix E)

Small group activities (explained later in section)

Musical instruments for accompaniment—In our case, our music teacher laid out a variety of instruments and written suggestions for songs and oversaw the station to assist students. We stopped occasionally and listened and/or jumped to student performances on the instruments.

Application

Allow students to choose their centers and move from area to area at their own pace. However, stop occasionally and let students know how much time remains and check to see if they have been to all the centers. Remember to provide Swiss Balls for those who would normally be resting and waiting for a turn to jump. Choice really allows students to work at their own level at areas in which they are interested without embarrassment. The availability of lots of fun areas that they must use in a limited amount of time also develops time management skills. Your students will be truly engaged the entire time.

Swiss Ball Small Group Activities

Partner Balance Challenges

Tossing and Catching (a variety of sponge blocks and balls, soft dice, yarn, and medicine balls were available)

Charts with letters, numbers, and words (see chapter 17)

Closure

Meet in a large circle to share thoughts on what students enjoyed about the jump and bounce activity.

The Swiss Balls added that low-impact alternative I was looking for. All special needs students were actively engaged even if it meant sitting on a paraeducator's lap and bouncing along to the music. Everyone really had a great time! And since our jump, I have been thinking about how to incorporate the balls in a simpler manner. The traditional jump has teams of students with one child jumping at a time. The balls could be added for those students waiting for their turn to jump. This way they would get a rest from jumping and be able to work on bouncing, stretching, or strengthening.

PART III

Swiss Balls in the Curriculum

CHAPTER 12

DEVELOPING LESSON PLANS AND ASSESSING PROGRESS

The activities we've described in part II are great ways to include Swiss Balls in your curriculum. In this part of the book, we'll show you how to build from activities to lessons. This chapter starts off discussing your children's needs and assessing progress. Chapters 13 through 16 provide tested lesson plans at different grade levels, and chapter 17 brings in other classroom activities.

Getting Started With Young Children

To keep the curriculum developmentally appropriate, you must focus on each individual child. What drives the preschool child is a basic curiosity about the environment and the quest for meaning. The Swiss Balls provide a novel approach to answering these needs by keeping the learning environment stimulating.

The key to developing skills in young children is to focus on the process instead of the product. Let them explore and discover the ball first. Then add guided discovery teaching strategies by asking "Can you . . . ?" questions and allowing them to try. Then, when they are more familiar with the ball, provide direct, but not command-style, instruction. How? Structure the learning environment to make it inviting and appropriate. Listen and learn from the children: they will tell you, in one form or another, what they find enjoyable or interesting. They will show you plenty of cognitive, affective, and physical skills that they are interested in exploring and refining.

The Cognitive Domain

Become familiar with the cognitive aspect of young children. Piaget's theory holds that young children actively construct their cognitive world through

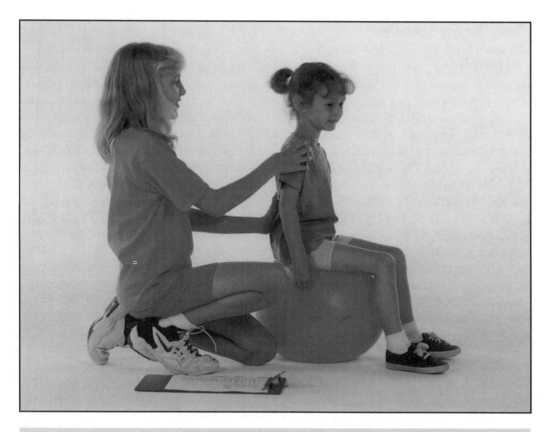

Young children benefit from detailed feedback, and may need extra help.

interaction with objects (1977). Most young children function in what Piaget calls the preoperational stage of cognitive development. This simply means they engage in symbolic thought (pretend play, one object representing another), are egocentric (cannot distinguish between their view and another's), and use intuitive thought (they just know what they know). So relate Swiss Ball activities to what is current and real in their world. For example, create lessons using themes such as the circus, colors and shapes, or a skill, such as balancing or rolling. Use concrete movement experiences to expand their movement vocabulary, asking questions such as, "What part of your body is on the ball?" Define space clearly by using poly-spots, hula hoops, masking tape or other lines, and so on. Finally, use movement experiences to foster language development by asking them to verbalize what they're doing.

Beyond understanding this age group's general characteristics, consider the different learning styles of children. Phyllis Weikart suggests presenting information using one method at a time (1987a). If you are demonstrating a skill, do not talk at the same time, and vice versa. If you are guiding a child by moving her through a movement with your hands, do not talk with the child until after you've finished. This helps the child process information efficiently and effectively. In addition, kneel or squat so that your eyes are level with the child's eyes when talking and demonstrating. Finally, take into account Gardner's Theory of Multiple Intelligences when designing lessons (see chapter 12).

The Affective Domain

Become familiar with the affective aspect of young children. Focus primarily on developing positive self-concepts. Child-initiated activities and situations in which you allow the children to make choices not only take into consideration developmental readiness, they also encourage children to personally invest in the activities. Give them many opportunities for success by using the Swiss Ball throughout the year, scaffolding (building on what they can do by themselves and assisting them to a higher skill level) their development, and keeping in mind the scope and sequence of the Swiss Ball curriculum.

Allow young children to develop a sense of responsibility about their bodies, behavior, and belongings. According to Erikson, young children's task for psychosocial development is initiative versus guilt (Santrock 1996). Developing a sense of responsibility will increase initiative. They're just learning to interact with others so you will see parallel play (playing next to each other but not interacting) with some sharing of ideas and balls with friends. Thus, it is developmentally appropriate to provide one Swiss Ball per child in small groups or learning centers, introducing partners or small group activities requiring ball sharing as challenges and extensions of self-play.

The Physical Domain

Be sure you're familiar with the physical characteristics of young children. The ball is a great way to experience crossing the frontal midline (front to back), the sagittal midline (horizontal), and the transverse midline (vertical), leading to readiness in the classroom. Moreover, they learn much about their environment simply by doing. "Movement experiences are the primary source for all learning by young children" (COPEC 1994). As you probably well know, it's not appropriate for them to sit and listen to a lengthy discussion about anything! They need to be touching and manipulating their environment and the things in it. So, ensure you create an environment in which children may be active most of the time. Provide, however, short recovery periods between vigorous activity bouts.

Keep the environment safe by providing wide, open spaces and enforcing simple safety rules. Appropriate rules for preschool children through adults include the following:

1.   Keep the ball under control—no silly stuff (throwing the ball at another person, kicking the ball aimlessly, bouncing it out of control) and stay in your own ball space (with help from poly-spots, carpet squares, or the like).

2.   Keep the body under control—no silly stuff, keep bounces on the ball small, slow, and controlled, and stay in self-space.

3.   Protect your head, especially when lying on your stomach on the ball. It is not OK to "bonk" your head on the floor (see Falling, a variation of Activity 5.18).

Keep in mind that young children need structure in order to feel and be safe. Give an overview of all the safety rules and then emphasize specific ones for a particular lesson. It is helpful to post the rules with accompanying pictures on the wall and refer to them as needed. Frequently ask the children for their suggestions of important rules when working with the balls; they will be delighted to take some ownership of the rules.

Other Considerations

Make each session a fun, enjoyable experience. Make the environment inviting by keeping equipment at their level with lots of variety and choices. Make it easy for them to put the equipment back where they found it to begin teaching personal responsibility. Always consider the ability and interest level of the individual. Support children's learning and help them to get to the next level of development by being interested in what they are doing and asking appropriate questions (e.g., "I wonder what happens if. . . ?") or making appropriate comments (e.g., "You found a different way to balance on the ball!").

Although age is an important factor to consider, remember, skill development is not entirely age-dependent. A three-year old child may be able to coordinate alternating arms with bouncing on the ball while a five-year-old may struggle with the Basic Bounce. So offer individualized challenges and extensions as appropriate.

In the rest of this chapter, we'll describe a progression of lessons we have found to be successful with preschool and kindergarten students. We'll outline both learning center and half class formats. No matter which format you use, however, it is best to review key concepts and introduce new lessons as a whole group. Feel free to adapt these lessons to suit your students' needs. Finally, we have listed the activities by number so you can easily refer to them in the developmental skill chapters (chapters 5 through 11).

Child-Directed Learning

As described in chapter 2, introduce the Swiss Ball in one of a few learning centers so you can concentrate on a few children at a time. Make sure the other centers involve activities that are already familiar to the children and easy to perform independently. Offer activities in which the children have expressed an interest. It is always important to have enough equipment at each center to insure maximum time on task vs. waiting for a turn or arguing over equipment. A learning center format is developmentally appropriate as it allows young children to choose their activities instead of being forced to do something they are either not ready for or not interested in.

Young children's interests are varied enough so that usually there are enough choices and equipment to meet their needs without having to share or wait their turn. However, if you find that there are too many children at one center, you can suggest ways in which they can take turns ("Do you think each person's turn should be two minutes or three minutes?") or invite them to the other centers. Let them be responsible for their choices. When explaining the ball center, address one or two skills and the safety rules for those skills. Taking the time to talk about the skills not only increases safety and performance, it also adds to the children's movement vocabularies.

Assessing Student Progress

Assessment is an important component of the learning process, and Swiss Ball learning is no exception. Specifically, we believe that all students can achieve success in Swiss Ball activities and that assessment will reinforce this success. How? Assessments help students take responsibility for practicing and perfecting the movements they are learning, giving them ownership of the learning process. They also define appropriate form and keep students accountable for striving for that form. Students will strive for excellence if you give them a blueprint to follow. Properly formulated assessment tools should be those blueprints.

The assessment worksheets at the end of this chapter are for assessing students' physical progress and achievement. The first form is a checklist for teachers, but the other forms are designed as worksheets for students. As both assessment and task sheets, these worksheets help students focus on the specific mechanics of the exercises. You can elect to have students either self-assess or peer assess. It may be useful to make an overhead transparency of each sheet as a visual aid to help explain what students are required to do. In addition, as students enjoy seeing sample drawings, these worksheets will inspire them to do their best.

Finally, we have included one question or topic on each worksheet that speaks to Gardner's Theory of Multiple Intelligences, allowing students to express their thoughts and feelings by drawing or writing (Gardner 1993; Armstrong 1994). If an assessment activity involves having students draw, post finished products to encourage good work and generate excitement. The APENS guidelines, especially 10.02 and 10.04, discuss standards for adapting assessment to children with special needs (APENS 1995). These worksheets are just examples to start the assessment process. Be creative!

Lesson Planning and Gardner's Theory of Multiple Intelligences

Gardner's Theory of Multiple Intelligences has become an important area to address when developing curriculum. The following are some of the ways we have addressed this theory with the Swiss Ball curriculum. Examine your teaching practices so students have frequent opportunities to learn and be assessed in all seven intelligences, can learn through a preferred intelligence, and can strengthen other intelligences.

Obviously, Swiss Ball activities address bodily-kinesthetic intelligence. We address the other intelligences in a variety of ways. Be sure to incorporate these and other activities to address all seven intelligences systematically in your lessons and units.

Linguistic: Use the written word on

- posters,
- task sheets, and
- assessment sheets.

Logical-mathematical: Develop through

- sequencing movements and
- counting patterns.

Spatial: Encourage through examining

- charts and
- drawings (posters).

Musical: Foster through

- rhythm,
- coordination, and
- folk dance.

Interpersonal: Develop through interpersonal interaction during work times as in

- cooperative learning activities and
- peer teaching opportunities.

Intrapersonal: Encourage through

- independent practice times,
- self-paced instruction,
- individualized projects, and
- choice times.

The worksheets will be useful during Swiss Ball lessons or any time during the school year to introduce these concepts to your students. They help students focus on each of the seven intelligences and recognize and acknowledge the different ways they are smart. If you think about these different areas of intelligence regularly and plan your lessons to touch on as many areas as possible, you will be enriching and enhancing the educational experience for all students.

Theme Format Assessment Worksheets

The sample worksheets at the end of the chapter focus on five different themes: balance, flexibility, muscular strength, cardiorespiratory fitness, and complete workouts. Use the easy-to-follow format to streamline your assessment efforts. Simply have students self- or peer assess by checking off one of three boxes, designating whether they can perform the skill correctly, almost have it, or need work. The questions at the bottom of these worksheets allow the child to go a little deeper through drawing or explaining what they have learned or enjoyed or how they think they can expand a skill or practice it in other ways.

Balance Assessment

Use the worksheets described in this section for peer or self-assessments after teaching specific balance activities (chapter 5) or during a fitness theme unit (since balance is a basic part of using Swiss Balls).

NASPE Standards (1995) for Balance (adapted)

Standard 1, benchmark for kindergarten: Maintains momentary stillness bearing weight on a variety of body parts.

Standard 1, benchmark for second grade: Balances, demonstrating momentary stillness, in symmetrical and asymmetrical shapes on a variety of body parts.

Standard 1, benchmark for fourth grade: Balances with control in a variety of positions on the Swiss Ball.

Standard 1, benchmark for sixth grade: Designs and demonstrates a series of balance positions on the Swiss Ball.

The Balance Assessment worksheet (figure 12.1) works well with first through third graders. Have students check whether they can or cannot perform the skill. Have pencils, clipboards, or a space on a bench to draw on and crayons ready so students can complete the worksheet, including the final question. Most students will finish this activity in three to five minutes. Allow students who wish to spend more time drawing to take the sheet home or back to class to finish.

Muscular Strength Assessment

Use these muscular strength worksheets as self-, peer, and teacher assessments with kindergarten through sixth grade students while teaching the activities in chapter 9 or during a fitness unit.

NASPE Standards (1995) for Muscular Strength (adapted)

Standard 4, benchmark for kindergarten: Lifts and carries a light weight such as the Swiss Ball.

Standard 4, benchmark for second grade: Supports body weight in a variety of weight-bearing postures with the Swiss Ball.

Standard 4, benchmark for fourth grade: Engages in appropriate activity that results in the development of muscular strength.

Standard 4, benchmark for sixth grade: Correctly demonstrates activities designed to improve and maintain muscular strength.

As with the flexibility worksheet, the Muscular Strength worksheet (figure 12.2) shows four different Swiss Ball activities to develop muscular strength. This worksheet can also be adapted for your needs based on the activities that you are emphasizing in your Swiss Ball curriculum.

Whole Class Format

If you are fortunate enough to have enough Swiss Balls for the whole class, you have several choices as to how to integrate them into your assessments and curriculum.

1. Have the entire class use the learning center format lessons simultaneously as short segments of a total lesson.
2. Combine two Swiss Ball lessons for a longer segment and create a manipulatives lesson from chapter 10 for a lesson comprised completely of Swiss Ball activities.
3. After teaching Lesson One and Lesson Two in each unit, use the balls for an aerobic warm-up at the beginning of class. Use only previously taught exercises, add music, and make up different sequences to perform to the music. Teach a few new exercises at the end of the warm-up to use in the next lesson's warm-up.
4. Use the Swiss Balls for a flexibility segment of a lesson.
5. Use the Swiss Balls for a strength segment of a lesson.

6. Create a Swiss Ball exercise circuit: Tape up enough posters of the different Swiss Ball exercises, so everyone can be at a different poster. Put on music, practice for 30 seconds, stop, and move to the next poster (holding the Swiss Ball over the head). Alternate balance, coordination and rhythm, strength, and flexibility exercises when setting up the circuit.

7. Set up four Swiss Ball task stations, such as foot motions, prone activities, partner activities, and strength activities. Have students spend one-fourth of the class period at each of the stations, working on specific exercises. Use previously learned exercises and be sure to tape posters at each station. You can also teach new exercises at one of the stations.

8. Use the Swiss Balls for folk dances.

Summary

We know the first few times you try a new assessment technique, it can be a little scary. Some teachers think students will not want to write anything during physical education. We have found quite the opposite to be true. Students are often eager to write or check off what they know how to do; they also take a great deal of pride in their written and artistic accomplishments. Moreover, the student who may only excel in body-kinesthetic activities will finally have a chance to write about something he or she is good at. Finally, well-designed assessments used in a timely fashion are *learning* tools, helping guide students toward better understanding of the content you're teaching. So use the examples in this chapter to help tailor your assessments to your situation, thereby enhancing skill acquisition for all students—no matter their strengths and weaknesses.

Name _____ Class _____ Date _____

Things I can do on the ball: Please check √ the box.

1.   Yes □   No □

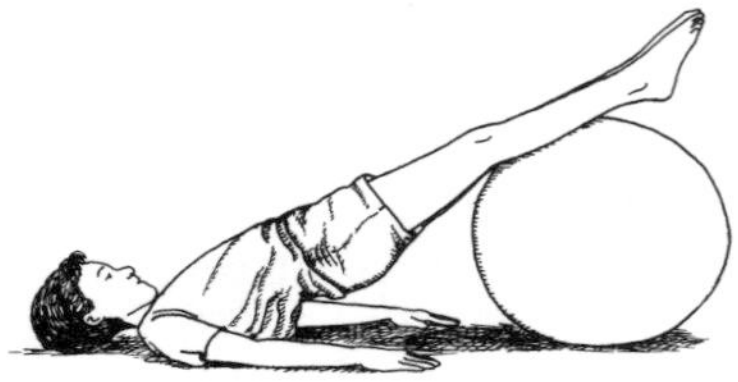

2.   Yes □   No □

3.   Yes □   No □

Please draw pictures of your favorite activities to do on and with the ball.

Figure 12.1   Balance Assessment worksheet.

Name _____ Class _____ Date _____

Muscular Strength: The force that a muscle or group of muscles can generate.

Please check the ☐ that indicates how you are doing so far.

1.

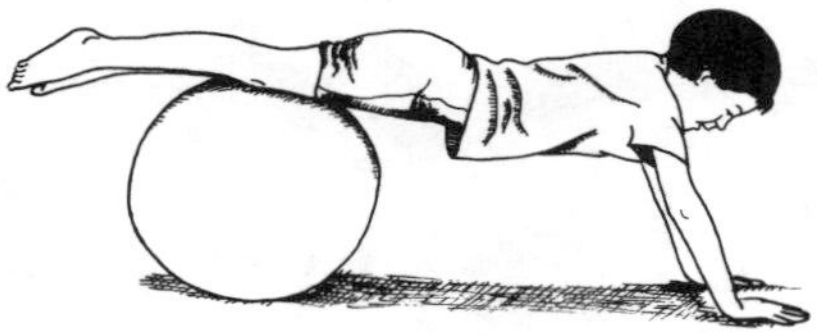

Achieved ☐

Almost ☐

Needs work ☐

2.

Achieved ☐

Almost ☐

Needs work ☐

3.

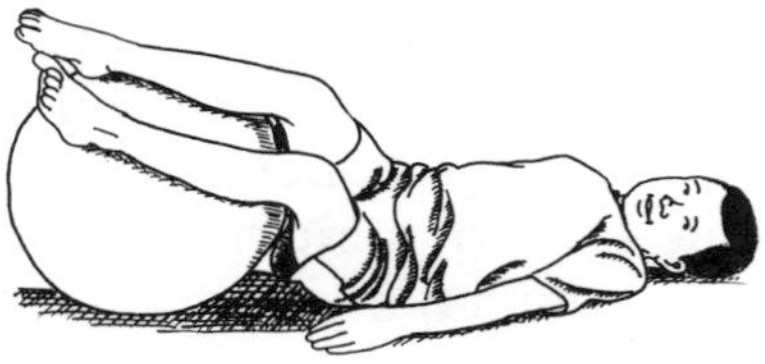

Achieved ☐

Almost ☐

Needs work ☐

4.

Achieved ☐

Almost ☐

Needs work ☐

Please list or write about other activities you are doing to increase your muscular strength.

Figure 12.2 Muscular Strength worksheet.

CHAPTER 13

LESSON PLANS FOR PRESCHOOL AND KINDERGARTEN

Three- to six-year-old children need a solid foundation of fundamental motor skills and a functional understanding of movement concepts that will lead to more complex skills later in their development. When teaching this age group, our philosophy is to give them the opportunity to learn and provide proper instruction and ample practice time. Skills and concepts progress from easy to complex, keeping all aspects of the child in mind: physical, affective, and cognitive. We advocate exploration and guided discovery as the main teaching strategies since most of these children are in the precontrol level of skill development. Some of the ideas included here have come from working with children and expanding on their responses and ideas.

Even very young children can use Swiss Balls in a classroom setting.

LESSON ONE: INTRODUCING THE SWISS BALL

Objective

To introduce the Swiss Ball, including safety, Sitting Correctly on the Ball (Activity 5.7), and the Prone Balance (Activity 5.17).

Equipment

Per student at Swiss Ball learning center: Swiss Ball, deck tennis ring (or the like), and floor marker.

Organization

Main format: learning center

Group size: 3-4 children

Time: 15-20 minutes

Setup: Set up balance-oriented centers around the gym (e.g., balance beam, balance boards, Swiss Balls, stilts). For Swiss Ball learning center, place balls on deck tennis rings (or the like), and scatter floor markers, three to four feet apart.

Set Induction

Introduce safety rules to whole group. Then define balance. Good balance means holding still, staying on, and not wiggling, wobbling, or falling. Discuss and demonstrate activity ideas for each balance-oriented learning center. Allow children to return to their center choices.

Procedure

Teach the following at the Swiss Ball learning center:

1. Introduce Sitting Correctly on the Ball (Activity 5.7)—young children will need to be reminded to keep feet on the floor and in front of the ball (have them put their feet on the floor marker in front of the ball). Check for correct ball size.

2. Introduce bouncing on the ball (chapter 6)—doing the Basic Bounce (Activity 6.1) with small bounces, staying in self-space (use floor markers), and practicing the Check Stop (Activity 6.2).

3. Introduce Prone Balance (Activity 5.17)—keep head from touching the floor.

4. Review safety rules.

Assessment

Check each student individually for safe behavior and correct technique.

Closure

Have children place all equipment back where they found it. During circle time, ask, "What was the name of the skill we practiced today?" Then assess affective domain by saying, "If you had fun during movement time today, carefully walk backward to the door."

LESSON TWO: MORE ON BALANCE

Objective

To review Lesson One and add more suggestions for sitting correctly; to introduce Prone Rocking (Activity 5.18).

Equipment

Per student at Swiss Ball learning center: Swiss Ball, deck tennis ring (or the like), and floor marker.

Organization

Main format: learning center

Group size: 3-4

Time: 15-20 minutes

Setup: Set up several centers around the gym. For Swiss Ball learning center, place balls on deck tennis rings (or the like), and scatter floor markers, three to four feet apart.

Set Induction

Review with the whole class the definition of balance, Sitting Correctly on the Ball, Basic Bounce, Prone Balance, and safety. Review and add activity ideas for each learning center (use child-initiated activity ideas from the previous class). Let the children choose the activities they are interested in, moving to stations at will.

Procedure

Teach the following at the Swiss Ball learning center:

1. Review and practice Sitting Correctly on the Ball (Activity 5.7)—ask, "Are you sitting tall? Are your feet staying on the floor? Are your feet in front of the ball?"
2. Review and practice Basic Bounce (chapter 6)—practice small bounces and the Check Stop (see Activities 6.1 and 6.2).
3. Introduce Prone Rocking (Activity 5.18).

Assessment

Check each student individually for safe behavior and correct technique.

Closure

Have children place all equipment back where they found it. During circle time, ask, "Did you have fun during your movement time today? Are you hot and sweaty?"

LESSON THREE: ROLLING AND CATCHING

Objective

To introduce the skills of rolling and catching.

Equipment

Per student at Swiss Ball learning center or centers: Swiss Ball, deck tennis ring (or the like), floor marker, and a variety of different-sized balls (such as beach balls, large foam balls, or rubber multi-purpose balls).

Organization

Main format: whole group, then learning center

Group size: 3-4

Time: 15-20 minutes

Setup: Set up several centers around the gym. For Swiss Ball learning center or centers, place balls on deck tennis rings (or the like), and scatter floor markers, three to four feet apart. Place smaller balls in containers near Swiss Balls.

Set Induction

Introduce the following to the whole class:

1. Define rolling—the ball is pushed and remains on the floor.
2. Define catching—stopping the ball with just the hands.
3. Allow children to make choices and explore at centers.

Procedure

Review the following at the Swiss Ball learning center:

1. Roll (Activity 10.1)—by self or with partner or small group.
2. Catch (Activity 10.5)—with a partner or small group.

Assessment

Check each student individually for safe behavior and correct technique.

Closure

Have children place all equipment back where they found it. During circle time ask, "What skills did you practice today using the balls? Did you enjoy playing with a friend today?" Then assess the affective domain by saying, "Walk back to back to the door with one other person you enjoyed playing with today."

Guided Discovery and Teacher-Directed Learning

After a few introductory lessons exploring the ball, young children may be ready for guided discovery and other teacher-directed activities. But, remember, young children need close supervision and individual attention to get the most out of a lesson. To organize guided discovery and teacher-directed activities, divide the class into halves. Have one half work at learning centers under the supervision of a classroom teacher or aide and the other half work under direction of the physical education teacher in small groups. Have the two groups switch halfway through the allotted time or for the next class session so that everyone gets to do all the activities.

LESSON FOUR: DROP AND STOP

Objective

To introduce the manipulative skills of Drop and Stop (catch).

Equipment

Per student at Swiss Ball learning center: Swiss Ball, deck tennis ring (or the like), and floor marker.

Organization

Main format: learning center

Group size: 3-4

Time: 15-20 minutes

Setup: Set up several centers around the gym. For Swiss Ball learning center, place balls on deck tennis rings (or the like), and scatter floor markers, three to four feet apart.

Set Induction

Discuss and demonstrate activity ideas for each learning center. Tell the children that they will put their hands, not their bodies, on the ball today. Let the children choose the activities they are interested in, moving to stations at will.

Procedure

Teach the following at the Swiss Ball learning center:

1. Review safety tips: Stay in self-space and keep the ball under control.

2. Introduce and practice the Drop and Stop (variation of Activity 10.5).

Assessment

Check each student individually for safe behavior and correct technique.

Closure

Have children place all equipment back where they found it. During circle time, ask, "Name the two types of bounces we practiced today. Did you like playing with others or by yourself today?" Then assess the affective domain by saying, "Walk to the door with one friend if you enjoyed playing with others today."

LESSON FIVE: PRONE ACTIVITIES

Objectives

To review safety, Prone Balance (Activity 5.17), Prone Rocking (Activity 5.18), and introduce Falling (variation of Activity 5.18) and the Prone Walk-Out (Activities 5.20, 9.9).

Equipment

Per student in half of class using the Swiss Balls: Swiss Ball, deck tennis ring (or the like), and floor marker.

Organization

Main format: half class

Group size: 6-8

Time: 15 minutes

Setup: Contain balls for one half of the class in one storage area and arrange floor markers in an activity area, three to four feet apart. The children will get the balls from the storage area and carry them to the activity area.

Set Induction

Review safety, balance, bouncing, and prone rocking. Introduce organization of the lesson. Have students carry balls from storage areas to floor spots.

Procedure

Teach the following at the Swiss Ball learning centers:

1. Practice Prone Balance and Prone Rocking.
2. Introduce and practice Falling, a variation of Prone Rocking.
3. Introduce and practice the Prone Walk-Out.

Assessment

Check each student individually for safe behavior and correct technique.

Closure

Have students place all equipment back where they found it. During circle time, ask, "What was your favorite activity with the balls today?" To assess the affective domain, say, "Walk to the door with one friend if you enjoyed playing with others today."

Summary

The lessons described here were specific to themes and should be prefaced with exploration. You should allow young children to explore when introducing the Swiss Balls as a new center—let them bounce, roll, kick, and dribble the balls. Some will want to sit, bounce, or be prone on the balls. If a student chooses to put their body on the ball, make sure the ball is the correct size. Let the students show you what they are interested in pursuing. Then in the next class session you can use those suggestions and focus their exploration as necessary. For example, "Today you may not put your body on the ball. The Swiss Balls are used only for rolling now."

Remember to focus on development of the fundamental motor skills and concepts when creating a lesson for young children. Once the basic skill is mastered, add challenges and extensions to help students move to the next level of development in all aspects—social, emotional, physical, and cognitive. Expand lessons to include all the content areas noted in this book (fitness, rhythm, etc.). Progress from simple to complex, selecting increasingly difficult elements and variations from the skill development chapters. Continue to develop more lessons by observing and listening to your students. Are they ready for more of a challenge with one skill or do they want to practice a totally new skill? Review and repeat a total lesson or part of a lesson. Young children will enjoy showing you and other students what they know or remember. Let them "teach" another student the correct way to do the skills. Take advantage of this time for authentic assessment.

CHAPTER 14

LESSON PLANS FOR FIRST AND SECOND GRADES

LESSON ONE: INTRODUCTION TO THE SWISS BALL

Objective

To introduce the Swiss Ball, safety, sitting correctly, and beginning coordination activities.

Equipment

Per student at Swiss Ball learning centers: Swiss Ball, deck tennis ring (or the like), floor marker.

Organization

Main format: learning center

Group size: 3-4

Time: 8-10 minutes

Setup: Set up centers around the gym. For Swiss Ball learning centers, place balls on deck tennis rings, and scatter floor markers, three to four feet apart.

Set Induction

Introduce or review how to use the ball safely (chapter 3) and Activity 5.7, Sitting Correctly on the Ball. Safety rules:

- Protect brain and spine through controlled movement.
- Work in self-space to prevent collisions.
- Use a correctly sized ball.

Children enjoy adding new skills.

Procedure

Introduce the following activities in the order listed:

1. Hold the ball lightly and begin bouncing gently. Bounce for about 16 counts until hearing the stop command.
2. Check Stop (Activity 6.2)—Explain that the Check Stop is an important safety measure because it helps a person maintain control. Practice.
3. The following activities are good beginning coordination activities. Introduce them one at a time and continue to practice the Check Stop to help students learn to maintain control. Have anyone out of control (wild bouncing or jumping feet from floor) put the ball back on the deck tennis ring and sit on the floor marker for a short time-out. This will help them remember to use smaller bounces and more control.

   - Basic Bounce (Activity 6.1)
   - Ball Taps (variation of Activity 6.1)
   - Thigh Pats (variation of Activity 6.1)
   - Push (Activity 6.4)
   - Lift (Activity 6.5)

Assessment

Check each student individually for safe behavior and correct technique.

Closure

Roll balls to deck tennis rings and have students sit on floor markers. Review how to use Swiss Balls safely. Then assess the affective domain by saying, "If you had fun during movement time today, carefully walk backward to the door."

LESSON TWO: FLEXIBILITY AND STRENGTH

Objective

To review the concepts covered in Lesson One and learn beginning flexibility and strength activities in prone position.

Equipment

Per student at Swiss Ball learning centers: Swiss Ball, deck tennis ring (or the like), and floor marker.

Organization

Main format: learning center

Group size: 4-5

Time: 10-15 minutes

Setup: Set up centers around the gym. For Swiss Ball learning centers, place balls on deck tennis rings (or the like), and scatter floor markers, three to four feet apart.

Set Induction

Review safety rules, correct sitting position, and coordination activities from Lesson One. Remind students how to select a correctly sized ball.

Procedure

1. Prone Rocking (Activity 5.18)—Students love this, so allow plenty of time for it.
2. A simple stretch (choose from Activities 8.1 through 8.4)
3. Prone Push-Up (Activity 9.9, variation)

Assessment

Check each student individually for safe behavior and correct technique.

Closure

Have children place all equipment back where they found it. During circle time, discuss flexibility and strength concepts as they relate to today's activities with the ball. Then assess the affective domain by saying, "If you had fun during movement time today, walk with a friend to the door."

LESSON THREE: COORDINATION AND BALANCE

Objective

To review coordination activities and practice balance activities.

Equipment

Per student at Swiss Ball learning centers: Swiss Ball, deck tennis ring (or the like), floor marker.

Organization

Main format: learning center

Group size: 4-5

Time: 8-10 minutes

Setup: Set up centers around the gym. For Swiss Ball learning centers, place balls on deck tennis rings (or the like), and scatter floor markers, three to four feet apart.

Set Induction

Review safety and coordination activities covered in Lesson One and Lesson Two.

Procedure

1. Introduce and have students practice the following coordination activities:
   - Wings (Activity 6.6)
   - Windshield Wipers (Activity 6.7)
   - Rainbow (variation of Activity 6.7)
2. Introduce and have students practice the following balance activities:
   - Balance practice (Activities 5.7, 5.8)
   - Seated Rocker (Activity 5.16)

Assessment

Check each student individually for safe behavior and correct technique.

Closure

Have children place all equipment back where they found it. During circle time, have students share their favorite activity. Then assess the affective domain by saying, "If you had fun during movement time today, clap your hands while you walk to the door."

LESSON FOUR: BALANCE, COORDINATION, AND STRENGTH

Objective

To practice balance, coordination, and strength activities on the Swiss Ball.

Equipment

Per student at Swiss Ball learning centers: Swiss Ball, deck tennis ring, and floor marker.

Organization

Main format: learning center

Group size: 4-5

Time: 10-15 minutes

Setup: Set up several centers around the gym. For Swiss Ball learning centers, place balls on deck tennis rings (or the like), and scatter floor markers, three to four feet apart.

Set Induction

Review safety issues, including correct sitting position, selecting the right ball size, and staying in self-space.

Procedure

1. Demonstrate and practice arm and hand balance positions:
   - Sitting Correctly on the Ball (Activity 5.7) hand position variations: resting hands on the ball and resting hands on thighs.
   - Basic Arm Movements (Activity 5.9), including the variations of Arms Overhead and Asymmetrical Arms.
2. Do these balance and arm movements in a quick game of Simon Says, Follow the Leader, or Mirroring.
3. Introduce and have students practice the following coordination activities while bouncing: Shoulder Taps (Activity 6.9), including Reach-Up and "L" Arms.
4. Review the Seated Rocker (Activity 5.16), which is the beginning stage of abdominal strength work.

Assessment

Observe individual students to assess balance. Note which students wobble or wave arms about for balance.

Closure

Have children place all equipment back where they found it. During circle time, have individuals share which balances were the most difficult or easiest for them. Then assess the affective domain by saying, "If you had fun during movement time today, hold your hand over one eye while you carefully walk to the door."

LESSON FIVE: RHYTHM—BEAT COMPETENCY

Objective

To enhance beat competency with an activity on the ball.

Equipment

Per student at Swiss Ball learning centers: Swiss Ball, deck tennis ring, and floor marker. Appropriate music (see dicussion in chapter 7).

Organization

Main format: learning center

Group size: 4-5

Time: 8-10 minutes

Setup: Set up several centers around the gym. For Swiss Ball learning centers, place balls on deck tennis rings (or the like), and scatter floor markers, three to four feet apart.

Set Induction

Review safety issues, including correct sitting position, selecting the right ball size, and staying in self-space.

Procedure

Use Pattern One (Activity 7.2) and music for this lesson:

1. Practice the taps first without bouncing and without music.
2. Add the music without bouncing.
3. Practice the taps while bouncing without the music.
4. Add the music and do the taps and bouncing to the music.

Assessment

Note which students are unable to tap to the beat of the music.

Closure

Have children place all equipment back where they found it. During circle time, discuss when rhythm is beneficial in sport activities. Then assess the affective domain by saying, "If you had fun during movement time today, clap your hands to the beat of the music we listened to while you walk to the door."

LESSON SIX: BALANCE AND STRENGTH—PRONE ACTIVITIES

Objective

To improve balance and strength with activities on the Swiss Ball.

Equipment

Per student at Swiss Ball learning centers: Swiss Ball, deck tennis ring, floor marker, and one copy of blank muscular strength assessment (such as figure 12.2).

Organization

Main format: learning center

Group size: 4-5

Time: 8-10 minutes

Setup: Set up several centers around the gym. For Swiss Ball learning centers, place balls on deck tennis rings (or the like), and scatter floor markers, three to four feet apart.

Set Induction

Review Lesson Two's skills: Prone Rocking (Activity 5.18), stretching (Activities 8.1 through 8.4), and the Prone Push-Up (Activity 9.9, variation).

Procedure

Introduce and have students practice the following:

1. Prone Balance (Activity 5.17)
2. Airplane (Activity 5.19, variation)
3. Superman and Superwoman (Activity 5.21, variation)

Assessment

Use the blank strength assessment form and paste pictures of the Arm and Leg Lift, Airplane, and Superman and Superwoman exercises. Decide upon the length of time each exercise should be held (5, 10, or 15 seconds). Have students mark as appropriate, using self- or peer assessment.

Closure

Have the children place all equipment back where they found it. During circle time, discuss the importance of strength to health and fitness. Then assess the affective domain by saying, "If you had fun during movement time today, clap your hands while you walk to the door."

LESSON SEVEN: COORDINATION—FEET

Objective

To improve foot coordination with Swiss Ball exercises.

Equipment

Per student at Swiss Ball learning centers: Swiss Ball, deck tennis ring (or the like), and floor marker.

Organization

Main format: learning center

Set Induction

Review how to use the balls safely.

Procedure

1. Introduce and have students practice the following heel moves:
   - Heel Lift (Activity 5.10), including Heels Apart and Together
   - Heel Touch (Activity 5.12 variation)
2. Introduce and have students practice the following toe moves:
   - Toe Lift (Activity 5.11)
   - Front Toe Touch (Activity 5.12 variation)
   - Side Toe Touch (Activity 5.12)
3. Marching

Assessment

Check each student individually for safe behavior and correct technique.

Closure

Have children place all equipment back where they found it. During circle time, have students share their favorite exercises. Then assess the affective domain by saying, "If you had fun during movement time today, march to the door with a friend."

LESSON EIGHT: BALANCE, FLEXIBILITY, AND STRENGTH

Objective

To promote balance, flexibility, and strength using Swiss Balls.

Equipment

Per student at Swiss Ball learning centers: Swiss Ball, deck tennis ring (or the like), and floor marker.

Organization

Main format: learning center

Group size: 4-5

Time: 8-10 minutes

Setup: Set up several learning centers around the gym. For Swiss Ball learning centers, place balls on deck tennis rings (or the like), and scatter floor markers, three to four feet apart.

Procedure

Introduce and have students practice the following:

1. Tabletop Balance (Activity 5.22)
2. Back Arch (Activity 8.8)
3. Prone Push-Up (Activity 9.9, variation)
4. Side Balance (Activity 5.23)

Assessment

Check each student individually for safe behavior and correct technique.

Closure

Have children place all equipment back where they found it. During circle time, discuss the benefits of balance and strength to health and fitness. Go over which exercises increase strength and which exercises foster balance. Then assess the affective domain by saying, "If you had fun during movement time today, walk to the door with two friends."

Summary

Continue to develop more lessons by selecting increasingly difficult elements from the skill development chapters as your students master the previous exercises. Review or repeat lessons as necessary, depending on how students are acquiring the skills in each lesson. In addition, you can use each of the lessons in this chapter a second time for review and practice. Students can work on their own or use student leaders. Review lessons can also give you the time you need for assessment. Use a balance of self-assessment, peer assessment, and teacher assessment as well as a balance of different tools that speak to the seven intelligences to ensure authenticity.

CHAPTER 15

LESSON PLANS FOR THIRD AND FOURTH GRADES

LESSON ONE: INTRODUCTION TO THE SWISS BALL

Objective

To introduce students to safe procedures for using Swiss Balls.

Equipment

Per student at Swiss Ball learning center: Swiss Ball, deck tennis ring (or the like), floor marker, copy of evaluation sheet (such as figure 12.1). Poster or overhead transparency showing the figures in Activity 5.7 (Sitting Correctly on the Ball).

Organization

Main format: learning center

Group size: 6-8

Time: 8-10 minutes

Setup: Set up several centers around the gym. For the Swiss Ball learning center, place balls on deck tennis rings (or the like), and scatter floor markers, three to four feet apart.

Set Induction

Review how to use the ball safely (chapter 3). Then show a poster or an overhead transparency illustrating how to sit on the ball correctly (figure 5.7). Have students work alone or with a partner to find a ball that is the appropriate size. Use two pencils to show what a 90-degree angle looks like. Explain that this is the position their legs should be in when sitting on the ball. Then check to ensure each student is sitting correctly on the right

You can adapt Swiss Balls for many traditional games.

size ball. Prime the students for learning by saying, "Did you know that your muscles have memory? Well, they do! When you practice balancing you are teaching your body how to recover from a possible fall."

Procedure

Direct students to do the following to learn to balance with control on the ball:

1. Bounce gently without lifting your bottom off the ball.

2. Slow down and just feel what it is like to sit still on the ball.

3. Listen to the definition of balance: maintaining a body position or pose against the pull of gravity. (See figure 5.7.)

4. Show different balances with control. (If necessary, show them different movements with their hands and arms, such as both arms out or both to one side; then show feet and legs, such as lifting toes or one foot.)

5. Remember, control means keeping your body from moving too fast or falling.

6. Copy each other's balances or keep working to create new balances. (You may also choose the more direct route and show posters from chapter 5. We prefer a combination of the posters and student-initiated ideas.)

7. Remember, practice improves performance.

Assessment

Check each student individually for safe behavior and correct technique. Have students choose three balanced positions and practice holding each one for three seconds. Use a drum or other instrument to signal students to hold their first pose, then hold a second and third in unison. Join students and let one of them strike the drum or instrument for the change signal so the signaler can see what it looks like when everyone is holding a different pose. Use the balance assessment sheet from chapter 12 (figure 12.1).

Closure

Have children place all equipment back where they found it. Ask them for feedback about specific skills and activities that they enjoyed or learned.

LESSON TWO: MUSCULAR STRENGTH AND BODY CONTROL

Objective

To define muscular strength and demonstrate how it helps students to control their bodies on the Swiss Ball.

Equipment

Per student at Swiss Ball learning center: Swiss Ball, deck tennis ring (or the like), floor marker, muscular strength assessment sheet (figure 12.2), poster or overhead transparency of "Sitting Correctly on the Ball" (Activity 5.7).

Organization

Main format: learning center

Group size: 6-12

Time: 10-30 minutes

Setup: Set up several centers around the gym. For the Swiss Ball learning center, place balls on deck tennis rings (or the like), and scatter floor markers, three to four feet apart.

Set Induction

Review the poster entitled "Sitting Correctly on the Ball" and discuss safety and ball size selection. Before beginning lesson, check each student's sitting position and ball size. Prepare the students for the lesson by asking, "Did you know that the 1998 mens' Olympic ski team trained on Swiss Balls? They did, and they found many of the strength exercises on the balls to be challenging."

Procedure

1. Have students sit on the balls correctly.
2. Allow them to gently bounce while listening.
3. Introduce or review the muscles used to perform the exercises they have been working on.
4. Discuss how they are using muscles to maintain control of their bodies while listening and discussing.

5. Show students the muscular strength assessment sheet. Go over the definition of muscular strength: the force, push, or pull that a muscle or group of muscles can generate.

6. Show posters and demonstrate the Prone Push-Up (variation of Activity 9.9), different crunches, and other strength exercises of your choice from chapter 9.

7. Have students try the strength moves, using the posters as guides.

8. Offer hands-on assistance where needed so students can get into the correct positions or have partners help each other.

Assessment

You can have students fill out the muscular strength assessment sheet or save it for a review lesson when they have had more practice. But show it to them this lesson, to help guide their learning and prepare them for a future assessment.

Closure

Have children place all equipment back where they found it. Ask students for feedback about specific skills and activities that they enjoyed or learned. Have them define strength, speaking to the person sitting next to them. Then ask for a volunteer to give a clear definition of muscular strength.

LESSON THREE: STRETCHING

Objective

To teach students how to stretch their muscles using the Swiss Balls.

Equipment

Per student at Swiss Ball learning center: Swiss Ball, deck tennis ring (or the like), floor marker. Per class: flexibility posters from chapter 8. Make one copy each of figures 8.1 to 8.12.

Organization

Main format: learning center

Group size: 6-12

Time: 10-15 minutes

Setup: Set up several learning centers around the gym. For Swiss Ball learning center, place balls on deck tennis rings (or the like), and scatter floor markers, three to four feet apart. Have stretching posters from chapter 8 lying flat on the floor near you for Procedure section of lesson.

Set Induction

Review how to use the ball and do the strength moves safely. While students are sitting correctly on the balls, introduce the lesson by covering the following points:

• Discuss the five components of health-related fitness: muscular strength, muscular endurance, flexibility, cardiorespiratory fitness, and body composition.

- Explain that today's focus is on flexibility, which is the ability to move a joint through its specific range of motion.
- Daily life requires you to be able to reach for things up on shelves or across tables.
- Some people have a very long reach because they have participated in some sort of stretching routine regularly.
- Activities such as karate, gymnastics, dance, baseball, and others require a great deal of flexibility to participate without injury.

Have students briefly share any extracurricular activities they may have participated in that regularly included stretching.

Procedure

1. Hold up each flexibility poster in turn.
2. Demonstrate each stretch.
3. Review safety rules for stretching:
   - Stretch to the point of resistance not strain or pain.
   - Hold stretch static for 10-30 seconds—no bouncing to stretch further.
   - Discuss and demonstrate having students spot each other.
4. Have students try the stretches by following the illustrations on the posters at the Swiss Ball learning center.

Assessment

Move around and spot, support, and adjust students' positions to ensure they are safely getting the full benefit of each stretch.

Closure

Have children place all equipment back where they found it. Ask a volunteer to define flexibility. Have students discuss with a partner or a small group how their muscles felt during the stretches.

LESSON FOUR: AEROBIC ACTIVITIES

Objective

To teach students aerobic exercises using Swiss Balls.

Equipment

Per student at Swiss Ball learning center: Swiss Ball, deck tennis ring (or the like), and floor marker. Per class: stereo system and music with a good tempo for bouncing (see chapter 7).

Organization

Main format: learning center
Group size: 6-12
Time: 10-15 minutes

Setup: Set up several learning centers around the gym. For the Swiss Ball learning center, select activities from chapters 7 (see Activities 7.1 through 7.16), which develop rhythm skills, and 9 (see Activities 9.22, 9.23, and 9.24), which develop cardiorespiratory fitness. Make the diagrams into posters or overhead transparencies to help you teach the exercises.

Set Induction

Review safety precautions and how to sit on the ball correctly. Have students find their pulse. Explain that today they are going to work on cardio-respiratory fitness by raising their heart rates for an extended time.

Procedure

1. Use the ideas in Activity 9.22 for a warm-up.
2. Teach the moves you selected (see Setup) to students slowly and carefully, because they will be repeating them during games, dances, and partner routines.
3. When all students have learned these movements, add music and lead them through the exercises. It is good to repeat each one at least eight times. Students will enjoy counting along with you.
4. Have students take their pulses again.
5. Use the ideas in Activity 9.22 to have students cool-down.

Assessment

Check each student individually for safe behavior and correct technique. Ask students how the exercises feel and if the pace at which you are teaching and demonstrating is OK. Have students tell you if their pulse was faster after working out than when they first came in.

Closure

Have children place all equipment back where they found it. Have them share what new skills they learned and what their favorite activities were.

LESSON FIVE: DESIGNING AN EXERCISE ROUTINE

Objective

To design a sequence of Swiss Ball exercises into a routine.

Equipment

Per student at Swiss Ball learning centers: Swiss Ball, deck tennis ring (or the like), floor marker, and pencil, clipboard, or other writing surface. Per class: stereo system and music; a variety of Swiss Ball posters from this book. Optional: scarves, ribbons, streamers, and lummi sticks add a little extra pizzazz; have crayons or markers ready for drawing.

Organization

Main format: whole class or learning center

Group size: 6-25

Time: 15-35 minutes

Setup: Duplicate and mount a variety of Swiss Ball posters from this book. Categorize the posters according to their focus or hang them randomly around the gym. Sit on a ball yourself to get the poster-hanging height correct. If you do not have enough Swiss Balls to involve the entire class at once, set up other related learning centers around the gym.

Set Induction

Review how to use the Swiss Balls safely and sit on them correctly. Prepare the students for learning by saying, "Have you ever made up a jump rope, gymnastics, or dance routine? It is a sequence of at least 3 moves repeated 4 or more times each." Have a routine ready to show students on the ball. Demonstrate your routine and continue.

Procedure

1. Show students the posters.
2. Have them design a game, dance, gymnastics, or exercise sequence alone, with a partner, or in a small group. The sequence must have at least three different exercises, hold four counts, or be repeated four times.
3. Allow plenty of time for students to design and record their sequences. Allow students to take the form around the gym first and write down their choices or make up safe, controlled movements. Or let them take a ball with them and try out movements before writing them down.

Assessment

When students have completed their sequences, let them show them to you privately or to the group. Or videotape students who would like to see themselves. You can use these videotapes to demonstrate the concept of designing and performing a sequence to your other classes.

Closure

Have children place all equipment back where they found it. Then discuss how being involved in this activity felt. Discuss successes you have seen and have students share what they saw or more about how they felt. When viewing classmates' ideas, encourage students to clap to show their appreciation.

LESSON SIX: THROWING, CATCHING, AND HAND DRIBBLING

Objective

To practice the skills of throwing, catching and hand dribbling Swiss Balls.

Equipment

Per student at Swiss Ball learning centers: Swiss Ball, deck tennis ring (or the like), floor marker, basketball, rubber playground ball (8 1/2 inch). Per class: containers with a variety of small balls, including Nerf, yarn, and any others you feel are appropriate.

Organization

Main format: whole class or learning center

Group size: 6-25

Time: Part 1: 5-20 minutes; Part 2: 20-30 minutes (you can divide this lesson into two parts on the same day or when they fit into your curriculum)

Setup: For Swiss Ball learning centers, place balls on deck tennis rings (or the like), and scatter floor markers so they are 4 to 5 feet apart. Then set out containers with a variety of balls in them, including Nerf, yarn, and any other balls you feel are appropriate. If you do not have enough Swiss Balls to involve the entire class at once, set up other related learning centers around the gym.

Set Induction

Review how to use and sit on the Swiss Balls safely and correctly. Review throwing and catching key points: call the person's name, make eye contact, and throw the ball directly to the person's hands. Review the underhand and overhand throws while standing. Introduce how to throw and catch while sitting on the ball.

Procedure

Be sure these activities are very focused and controlled.

Part 1:

1. Allow students to work with a wall, partner, or group of three.
2. Let students choose two balls: one to throw and one to sit on.
3. If using a wall, have them pick a spot on the wall about chest-high. If working with others, have students extend their hands to make a target to throw at.
4. Have students throw underhand toward the target.
5. When they are successful, let them try the overhand throw.
6. Be sure they are throwing gently and accurately, because when the receiver is seated on a ball an inaccurately thrown ball is impossible to catch.
7. As long as they are on task, let groups add more students and have as many as three balls going at a time.

Part 2:

8. Introduce or review hand dribbling and passing a ball to a moving receiver with rubber playground balls. When students have mastered this, allow them to exchange the rubber ball for a basketball.
9. To practice this skill, have one group of students sit on the balls in a line, each dribbling a playground ball in front of them, slightly to one side.
10. Facing the first group, have a group of students without any equipment standing in a line. On your signal, have the standing group walk past the sitting and dribbling group. As the walkers pass, the seated students call their names and use either a chest pass, bounce pass, or overhead pass to get the ball to the person walking, who catches it and gently throws it back.
11. Challenge pairs who are ready to have the walker jog past.
12. Switch roles.

Assessment

Check each individual's skill progression. Give hands-on assistance as necessary and appropriate. Ask students to rate their own abilities to throw and catch while sitting on a Swiss Ball.

Closure

Have students discuss among themselves how they think they did and what they liked about the activities. Ask students if they feel any part of the lesson enhanced cardiorespiratory fitness. Discuss why or why not.

Summary

Continue to develop more lessons by observing and listening to your students. Their actions and comments will show whether they are ready for more of a challenge with one skill or to practice a totally new skill. Review and repeat a total lesson or part of a lesson. Young children will enjoy showing you and other students what they know or remember. Let them "teach" another student the correct way to do the skills. Take advantage of this time for authentic assessment.

CHAPTER 16

LESSON PLANS FOR FIFTH AND SIXTH GRADES

LESSON ONE: FOCUSING ON FITNESS

Objective

To improve cardioresiratory fitness, strength, and flexibility using Swiss Balls.

Equipment

Per student at Swiss Ball learning centers: Swiss Ball, deck tennis ring (or the like), and floor marker. Per class: fitness skills signs (flexibility figures 8.1 through 8.12, muscular strength figures 9.1 through 9.21, cardiorespiratory fitness figures 9.22 through 9.24) For a cardiorespiratory area, stethoscopes with alcohol swabs to clean ear pieces after every use or, if possible, heart rate monitors. Posters of exercises from chapters 8 and 9 (for example 8.1 through 8.12, 9.1 through 9.21 and 9.22 through 9.24). Signal (music, drum, or the like) to indicate when to move to next learning center.

Organization

Main format: learning center

Group size: 6-12

Time: 20-35 minutes for the entire lesson

Setup: Designate learning center areas by posting fitness category signs above the exercise posters. Place stethoscopes and alcohol swabs and, if you have them, heart rate monitors in the cardiorespiratory area. (Ensure students have been trained in the use of these in a previous lesson.)

Swiss Balls work well with other equipment.

For Swiss Ball learning center, place Swiss Balls on deck tennis rings (or the like), and scatter floor markers.

Set Induction

Review how to use the Swiss Balls safely. Specifically go over the following rules:

- Protect brain and spine through controlled movement.
- Work in self-space to prevent collisions.
- Use the correct size ball to safely perform all exercises.

Prepare the students for the lesson by asking, "Can you name all the components of fitness? Did you know that you can do all those using the Swiss Balls?"

Procedure

1. Use starting and stopping music or a drum beat to add excitement and to signal center changes.
2. Once students are working at centers, visit each student to be sure that they are performing the skills correctly.

Assessment

Check for understanding through discussion. Ask students to give examples of muscular strength and endurance, flexibility, and cardiorespiratory fitness exercises. Ask which they found particularly fun or challenging.

Closure

Have children place all equipment back where they found it. Ask students to name the four components of health-related fitness covered in today's lesson. Ask students for examples of how they can work on muscular strength and endurance, flexibility, and cardiorespiratory (aerobic) exercises in their daily lives. Briefly discuss the how these four components can help an individual improve the fifth component—body composition.

LESSON TWO: DESIGN AND PERFORM A DANCE

Objective

To design and perform a dance using the Swiss Ball.

Equipment

Per student at Swiss Ball learning centers: Swiss Ball, deck tennis ring (or the like). Optional: Scrap paper, pencils, and clipboards for those who want to draw or write down their dances. Per class: music, stereo system, and exercise posters from this book.

Organization

Main format: whole class or learning center

Group size: whole class or small groups

Time: 20-35 minutes

Setup: Post aerobic exercise diagrams (9.22 through 9.24 from this book) around the gym from which students may choose exercises. If you don't have enough Swiss Balls for everyone, create a Swiss Ball learning center by placing Swiss Balls on deck tennis rings (or the like), and scatter floor markers.

Set Induction

Review how to make safe, controlled movements on the ball. Teach students a folk dance from chapter 7 as a warm-up, such as Macarena (Activity 7.8), Alley Cat (Activity 7.12), Popcorn (Activity 7.13), or Bele Kawe (Activity 7.16).

Procedure

1. Tell students they are going to have the opportunity to change the dance by creating moves of their own design. Emphasize originality.

2. Explain the parameters of this task:
   - Work alone, with a partner, or in a small group.
   - Create or choose a minimum of three movements that go to the beat of the music.
   - Write or draw these movements on scrap paper.

3. Move around the room to be sure everyone is actively participating. As this activity may be difficult, focus on any individual or group who is struggling, giving more direct guidance and assistance. For example, do a simple dance you have made up with them to try to free them from some of their inhibitions.

Assessment

Have students turn in their written notes. Give students a chance to perform their dance moves on the ball for another individual or group if they wish.

Closure

Discuss the level of difficulty with your students. If appropriate, you might say, "Because we all have different ways that we are smart, some people who are 'music smart' found the activity easy, while others found it extremely difficult. It is very good for your brain to learn and practice things that you may find difficult. It is good to 'stretch' your brain in this way."

LESSON THREE: COOPERATIVE FITNESS WORKOUT

Objective

Students will work together cooperatively to choose and perform fitness exercises on the Swiss Balls.

Equipment

Per student at Swiss Ball learning center: Swiss Ball, deck tennis ring (or the like). Per class: stereo with music, exercise posters of your choice for warm-ups, aerobics, stretching, and strengthening exercises.

Organization

Main format: whole class or learning center

Group size: 3-6 students or whole class

Time: 20-35 minutes

Setup: Hang posters of various types of exercises so students can choose one if they cannot remember one. Decide if you would like to have students participate as a whole class or in small groups. If you are going to have them working in small groups, assign groups of three to six or allow students to choose whom they will work with. If you don't have enough Swiss Balls for everyone, create a Swiss Ball learning center by placing Swiss Balls on deck tennis rings (or the like), and scatter floor markers.

Set Induction

Review how to use the balls safely. Describe today's objective. Then, because the cooperation benchmark can be a tricky one to achieve, depending on the mixture of students in your room, take time to talk to students about verbal and nonverbal cooperation and how important it is to be respectful of others. Next, if you are allowing them to choose their groups, let them know they are responsible for being sure everyone is included and feels welcome. Role-play or brainstorm what cooperation looks like and sounds like.

Procedure

1. Form groups of three to six. Help them make this process a positive experience.
2. Start with slow music and have students take turns leading their groups in 6 to 12 repetitions of warm-up type exercises of their choice.

3. Have students continue to take turns as you call out which fitness category from which to choose an exercise. Have groups be sure everyone has an opportunity to lead.

4. Play slower music again for a cool-down.

Assessment

Check off names of students who share exercise demonstrations in your grade book in case you run out of time and you want to be sure to offer a chance to those who didn't get a turn to lead, but wanted to, at the start of the next lesson. Observe each individual for safe behavior and correct technique.

Closure

Have children place all equipment back where they found it. Compliment students on specific cooperative behaviors you observed, such as volunteering, following the leader respectfully, creating new exercises, and taking turns.

LESSON FOUR: ROLL YOUR WAY TO FITNESS

Objective

To reinforce math skills while using dice to decide how many times or how many exercises from each category to perform.

Equipment

Per student at Swiss Ball learning center: Swiss Ball, deck tennis ring (or the like). Per class: fitness exercise posters, small or large dice for partners or small groups, stereo system, and lively music (see chapter 7).

Organization

Main format: whole class or small groups

Group size: 6-30

Time: 20-35 minutes

Setup: Hang posters of various types of exercises so students can choose one if they cannot remember one. Decide if you would like to have students participate as a whole class or in small groups. If you are going to have them working in small groups, assign groups of three to six or allow students to choose whom they will work with. If you don't have enough Swiss Balls for everyone, create a Swiss Ball learning center by placing Swiss Balls on deck tennis rings (or the like), and scatter floor markers.

Set Induction

Review how to use the ball safely. Discuss responsible choices of partners with whom individuals can remain on task and productive. As this is a difficult concept, be ready to step in and assist as necessary to make this a positive and productive learning experience for everyone.

Procedure

1. Have students form partners or groups of three.

2. Teach the class how to play Roll Your Way to Fitness (Activity 11.4).

3. Give each group or pair a pair of dice.

4. Direct students to take the dice and their Swiss Balls around the room to exercise posters that are not crowded and take turns rolling the dice to see how many times to perform the exercise or how many seconds to hold the stretch.

5. Turn on the music to begin the game. If necessary, stop the music to clarify or modify instructions.

Assessment

During the lesson, observe each student individually for safe behavior and correct technique. Continue assessment during Closure activity.

Closure

Find out what students learned as well as what they need work on by asking questions such as the following:

- Did you make responsible decisions about using time?
- Do you think you make a wise decision about whom to work with?
- Did you remember the safety rules?
- Did you follow through with decisions made with your partner or group?
- Did you stay on task the entire time?
- Does anyone have suggestions for modifying the game the next time we play it?

Summary

We hope these lessons will have your program up and rolling. Do listen for student modifications and suggestions because they're gold mines!

CHAPTER 17

CLASSROOM EXPERIENCES AND SUGGESTIONS

In this chapter, we will discuss how and why the Swiss Balls were introduced into classroom settings in our own schools and specific strategies for introducing them into the classrooms in your school in a safe and controlled manner. Then, we will share the results of an informal survey we made of both classroom teachers and students who use Swiss Balls in their classrooms.

Our Ball History

Anne Spalding was intrigued by the balls and purchased six to use as a learning center in her physical education program. It did not take long for her to purchase more balls and begin to use them in a wide variety of ways. She consulted Joanne Posner-Mayer, a physical therapist, for more information on Swiss Balls and sensory integration. At the time, Anne was on a school-wide committee that screened children who were struggling with a variety of behavioral and academic problems in the classroom. She started thinking about how much Swiss Balls could help certain students who were having a hard time focusing and who, consequently, were disrupting their classrooms. She read several articles about the successful use of balls as chairs in classrooms in Switzerland and thought the balls might be the answer for overactive students who were struggling to focus and learn. So Anne lent a few balls to two colleagues, to begin using as chairs in their classrooms. The project grew as other teachers experimented with having one or two balls in their classrooms.

Adaptations

As discussed throughout this book, visual aids illustrating the correct sitting posture are essential. A correct sitting position increases both safety and enjoyment of all the benefits that naturally stem from good posture. Some students experience good posture for the first time when sitting on the ball, which can also open up the chest for easier and deeper breathing, consequently helping students be more alert. Thus, classroom teachers in our schools display posters similar to "Sitting Correctly on the Ball" (activity 5.7) so students have a regular reminder of how to align their bodies when sitting on the ball. Naturally, the children are excited and curious about having the balls in their classrooms.

Our test-piloting teachers learned that they needed a minimum of two balls for the students: one for the fidgety child and one to rotate among the rest of the students in the class. (Ensure that you follow the guidelines for ball size in chapter 3.) Teachers and students knew it was an experiment and that if things did not go well, the balls would simply go back to the gym. This certainty encouraged students to be on their very best behavior.

The following is a list of tested ways to rotate the balls:

- Have interested students write their names on the chalkboard and take turns.

- Have students earn the privilege as a way to modify behavior.

- Give each group of four a ball and have them decide how to share it fairly. This encourages clear communication and thoughtful cooperation—benefits that may carry over to other areas.

- Set or allow students to set a time limit for turns (e.g., one hour, half of a school day).

Naturally, some students initially had a little trouble controlling their behavior with such a new and exciting "chair." But soon everyone understood the following guideline: sitting on a ball in the classroom is a privilege the teacher will revoke if an individual disturbs the learning environment. So encourage the classroom teachers in your school to set clear guidelines in advance, then enforce their expectations consistently.

Excited about the benefits of the Swiss Balls, the classroom teachers soon added an exercise corner to their rooms. A set of exercise posters, a cassette player with headphones so students could listen to music with a steady beat while performing the exercises, and a ball were all they needed. The teachers consulted with Anne to help them choose exercises the children had already learned during physical education classes. The exercise corners helped "squirmy" students be more productive, because—as you probably well know—an exercise break wakes people up both physically and mentally. Remember, too, exercising on the Swiss Ball helps the overactive child calm down while it arouses the underactive child. Children without disabilities benefit, too.

Swiss Balls can be adapted to a wide range of students.

At Anne's new school, another classroom teacher, uses several balls as chairs in her room. Her class quickly learned responsible ball behavior, and she has adapted the balls' use in many ways. Peeking into her room, you must look carefully to even notice the balls, because the students are on task. This teacher has seen a big difference in the productivity and behavior of all her students and may soon expand to having as many as half her class "on the ball" at a time.

This experience is typical: you can hardly tell the balls are there after the first few days. Indeed, it does not take long for the novelty to wear off as the balls become a regular part of the classroom. In fact, when Anne needs the balls to teach her physical education classes, they are sorely missed, and students clap when she returns them! So think of the balls as relatively inexpensive, but therapeutic, furniture. Certainly, they are a good investment in the educational environment for *all* children.

Safety and Responsibility

Safety has always been every teacher's number one concern, and there are three big safety issues involved in adapting the Swiss Balls to classroom use: sitting correctly on them, preventing punctures, and avoiding excessive heat. Students should learn how to sit correctly on the balls in physical education, and, as mentioned, classroom teachers should display the "Sitting Correctly on the Ball" poster around the room (see activity 5.7). Then, brainstorm with students about all the sharp and potentially dangerous things they must keep away from the balls: pencils, pens, staples, tacks, pebbles, and "stickers" from certain plants as well as anything hot, including heater vents. Once students are aware of these hazards and the possibility that they will damage the balls, they will all be cautious so they can keep this exciting privilege.

Classroom Survey

As we introduced the Swiss Balls into the classroom setting, we surveyed both teachers and students. In this section, we will share what we have learned from their responses. Although our investigations have been informal, the results do shed some light on questions classroom teachers often have.

Teacher Feedback

All of the teachers we questioned liked having the balls in their classrooms. In general, teachers felt that when students first got on the balls they were more squirmy. But this tapered off, and they paid more attention to the tasks at hand while seated on the ball than they had in the past. They noted that students seemed to be motivated by the balls and looked forward to their turn on the ball. Overall, teachers felt that the students were calmer while sitting on the ball. Some teachers found that habits such as shirt sucking and hair twirling decreased while certain students used the balls. Most teachers found that students with hyperactive tendencies and attention deficit disorders could and should spend more time on the balls than other students. However, many teachers felt all students benefited all the time. In short, the benefits teachers noticed most often were greater integration of brain and body, better coordination, increased concentration, calmer students, stronger trunk muscles, improved academic achievement, more amiable behavior among students, and—of course—improved posture.

Here are several success stories:

• A second grade teacher in Aspen, Colorado, reports, "I told one child that I bought the ball especially for him and that it would help him improve his handwriting by helping his brain and body work together. His handwriting improved! He also had attention problems and would sit on the ball during class discussion, so even if he wasn't totally tuned in, at least he wasn't rolling on the floor."

• A learning disabilities teacher in Thornton, Colorado, explains, "I think the balls are one of the best purchases I ever made for my classroom. I have a videotape showing how useful they are for kids. It is a great way to show parents why we use them."

• A second grade teacher in Westminster, Colorado, says, "In our class, we have several students on Ritalin who have attention deficit disorder and hyperactivity plus numerous other special problems. As these conditions are now becoming the norm, teachers are looking at as many avenues as possible to help their students. The Swiss Balls help! Students tend to calm down and are more focused on what they are learning. Students gain more confidence in themselves. In the future, I would like to have a ball for everyone in our room—including one or two for guests!

Student Feedback

Classes of second, third, and fourth graders also gave us invaluable feedback. The majority liked sitting on the balls in the classroom, and they thought the balls helped them concentrate and made them feel calmer, helping them get their work done. When asked to explain why they did or did not like using the Swiss Ball, we got responses like these:

- "I like using the ball because it is fun."
- "I like the ball because it's bouncy and it gives you exercise."
- "I like it because it is comtherbal [comfortable]."
- "I liked it because you get calmed down."
- "I like using the ball because I can get my work done a lot better."
- "I would like to sit on a ball all the time."
- "I feel good."

Using an eye chart.

SPELLING, WORD FAMILIES, AND VOCABULARY

Appropriate Group

First, second, and third grade

Equipment Needed

Circle chart for spelling, word families, and vocabulary (figure 17.1). A pointer. Swiss Balls.

Procedure

Call the numbers from underneath the circles and have students make the sound and add that sound to the "it" in the center of the chart. These are words within words and students should catch on quickly.

Summary

As you can see, students and teachers alike love having the balls in the classroom. We hope that after reading this chapter you will feel comfortable adding a ball or two to your classroom. If you are a physical educator, suggest to some classroom teachers in your building that they give the balls a try. The possibilities are endless!

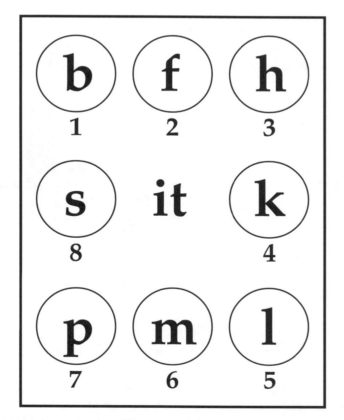

Figure 17.1   Circle chart for spelling, word families, and vocabulary.

MAINTENANCE AND STORAGE

You must plan for a place to store the balls. The balls will get dirty, and they may suffer punctures. This appendix suggests ways to store, wash, and screen them for punctures.

Storage Suggestions

There are many different ways to store the balls. You can use deck tennis rings to keep individual balls from rolling when not in use during classes, but if you are using several balls, choose one of the following storage methods to use between school days:

1. Use a prefabricated washer-dryer rack with the middle shelf lowered and shelves turned upside down so that lip is facing upward. The bottom shelf is optional.
2. Attach a prefabricated wire closet rack to a wall with "L" brackets. Choose a system that has an upward-turned lip to hold balls and physiorolls more effectively.
3. Hang nets, especially cargo nets, from the ceiling in a variety of ways. These will hold a large number of balls.
4. Parachutes are also great for storing large numbers of balls. You can gather them with sturdy clips (carabiners) and attach them to ropes that run through a pulley system suspended from the ceiling. The parachute illustrated holds over 30 balls.
5. Attach hoops to the wall to hold balls off the floor.
6. Store balls and step benches on shelving made of metal pipe. Stack the benches vertically.
7. Assemble PVC sprinkler pipe and connection joints to form cages. Or use other materials such as wood dowels and elastic tubing. Elastic tubing, also known as surgical tubing, offers an added advantage because it stretches to let balls out.

8. Make a ball cage with rubber or plastic cones to contain the balls between classes.

Maintenance

Use the tips in this section to keep the balls clean and check for potential damage.

Cleaning

"The great ball wash" is like a car wash for the Swiss Balls. If you are going to have a ball wash, we recommend recruiting parent volunteers. Not surprisingly, a ball wash can get messy, and it is best to have at least one other adult to help supervise students. You will need buckets of warm soapy water, clear water for rinsing, and rags or towels. Do not use abrasive or chemical cleaners on the balls. A mild dishwashing liquid such as Ivory or Simple Green works well. Be sure cleaning solution is approved for PVC products.

We have done a ball wash as a learning center. Surprisingly few students had actually washed a car, so we needed to explain the basics. We had to show them how to wring out towels and rags and how to keep washing, rinsing, and drying towels separate. If you choose this route, have no more than six or seven students at the center at any one time, and divide them into washing, rinsing, and drying groups. That way everyone has a specific responsibility, and each group of six or seven that comes to the center will clean approximately six or seven balls. As you can imagine, this cleaning process has proved to be very popular with students as well as an effective way to keep the balls clean.

Checking for Air Leakage and Punctures

If you suspect a ball is losing air, follow these tips to ensure safe equipment.

1. If the ball loses air, first check for air escaping through the plug by putting a few drops of water around it. Watch for air bubbles to appear through the water. If air is escaping through the plug area, try switching plugs. This usually stops a leak.

2. If the ball still loses air, check for a gouge or puncture. Inflate the ball until it is firm and take a very wet sponge or cloth and rub it over the surface of the ball. Listen for the hissing sound of air escaping as it comes in contact with the water. If the ball is punctured, *discard it*.

When pressure (weight) is applied to a punctured ball, the puncture may tear and the ball will collapse. Working on a punctured or repaired ball is dangerous, and responsibility for any resulting injury may fall on the teacher, therapist, or school. Remember, preventing punctures is the best route to long ball life (see tips in chapter 3).

APPENDIX B

HISTORY OF THE SWISS BALLS

The large balls originated in 1963 when Italian plastics engineer Aquilino Cosani, owner of Ledraplastic Toy Manufacturing Company, started producing them out of vanilla-scented vinyl instead of pungent rubber. However, it was an innovative physical therapist, Mary Quinton, in Switzerland who first used the balls for therapy treatments with neurologically impaired children. Another therapist, Dr. Susanne Klein-Vogelbach, then pioneered ball techniques for posture retraining and back pain rehabilitation. Maria Kucera, P.T., developed the largest collection of ball exercises and the first therapeutic exercise programs for people unable to participate in normal fitness activities.

Since the large balls could only be purchased in Switzerland, they got their nickname "Swiss Balls" and are widely known to rehabilitation professionals by that name. The Swiss Balls first found their way to the United States in the early 1970s through a few American therapists who went to Switzerland to learn from the pioneering Swiss therapists. It wasn't until the mid-1970s that the balls could be purchased in the United States and they were mostly used by therapists treating children with cerebral palsy.

Then in the late 1980s, due to the increasing number of people suffering from acute or chronic back pain and increased research, medical treatment for spine patients changed from bed rest and medication to light activity and spinal exercises. In 1986, Joe Montana, a football player for the San Francisco 49ers, underwent back surgery. His miraculous return to the game after only six weeks of rehabilitation received considerable national attention. His rehabilitation program included exercises using the Swiss Ball. Thus, American therapists began using this special ball more widely in the orthopedic arena.

In the spring of 1988, Vlatka Zeller, a Swiss therapist, concerned with the escalating numbers of teenagers with back pain, hypothesized that excessive sitting was responsible for the postural weakness and damage she saw in her patients. With the help of an elementary school doctor and principal, she introduced balls as a replacement for their traditional chairs thinking that sitting on a dynamic surface would prevent the back pain found in teenagers.

The success of this initial program led to a large scale test in Switzerland which showed that children sitting on balls produced the following results:

- Hyperactive children became calmer and could focus for longer periods.
- Other children could generally concentrate better.
- Handwriting skills improved for children with poor penmanship.
- Children often showed a better understanding of subject material.
- Disorganized children developed a better sense of organization. (Illi 1994)

A manual, *Sitting is Weight Bearing: We Sit Too Much* (1991), was created in a cooperative effort between Swiss physical educators and classroom teachers. Today, there are approximately 5,000 Swiss classrooms still sitting on balls and use of the balls has spread to other European countries to promote improved posture and physical activity while sitting.

In the early 1990s, therapists who were trained in Switzerland, including co-author Joanne Posner-Mayer, began introducing the Swiss Ball techniques not only to other physical and occupational therapists but also to US physical educators including the co-authors, Anne Spalding, Janet Santopietro, and Linda Kelly, along with classroom teachers, athletic trainers, and fitness professionals. Since that time, children in the US have been observed by their teachers to show the same positive effects from ball use as their Swiss counterparts. There have been several informal studies on the beneficial effects of balls in classrooms but no scientific studies have been published at the time of this printing. This book was developed by the authors to answer the many requests for information on how to implement a ball program into the school setting and provide a useful instructional resource for physical educators, classroom teachers, and therapists for the ultimate benefit of the children they influence.

Since the same Swiss Balls manufactured by Cosani over 25 years ago are still in use in rehabilitation facilities today, it is clear that they are built to last with proper care. An investment in Swiss Balls for your physical education program today may also benefit the children of tomorrow as you expand this pioneering field to include your school.

ANATOMY OF THE SPINE AND ITS STRUCTURES

Use the following information to help educate children about the anatomy of the spine. Adapt the content to fit students' grade level and abilities. Use plenty of visual aids such as the ones provided in this chapter.

The spine is made up of 24 bones called *vertebrae*, and the *sacrum* and *coccyx*, at which the hip bones and pelvis attach (see figure C.1). There are three dynamic (movable) curves in the vertebrae and one fixed:

1. Cervical-7 vertebrae
2. Thoracic-12 vertebrae
3. Lumbar-5 vertebrae
4. A fused curve for the sacrum and coccyx

These curves are what hold the head and trunk up against gravity in the most energy-efficient manner. Between each pair of vertebrae are thick, tough (*cartilaginous*) tissues called (*invertebral*) *discs*. The discs form round pillows sandwiched between the vertebrae, keeping the vertebrae from rubbing on one another and allowing movement between the bones.

Around the vertebrae and discs are other tough tissues called *ligaments* and *fascia*. (You might mention that when kids eat meat and find a tougher hard part that they can't chew, it is one of those tissues.) These structures all help keep the bones tightly together.

Surrounding these structures are muscles which give us the control to move our bones—or keep them still. First, small muscles (*multifidus*) extend from one vertebrae to another or are attached over three or four vertebrae. On top of those small, deep muscles are the large (*paraspinal*) muscles we can feel under our skin.

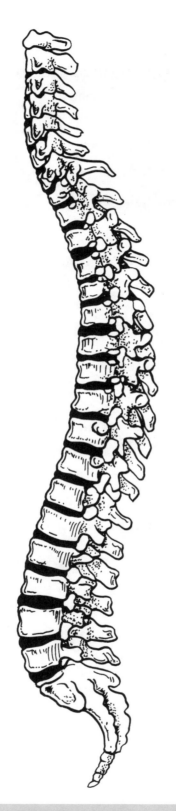

Figure C.1   Adult spine

To summarize, four things give our bodies shape, flexibility, and strength: the curves of the spine, the discs, the ligaments and fascia, and the muscles. In addition, these structures work together to help absorb shock caused by the force of gravity on our bodies when we walk, run, or jump.

Usually, as people age, the movement in their spine decreases due to the results of poor posture, gravity pulling them down, and compression of the discs between the vertebrae as the discs slowly lose their water content. As the discs become compressed, they help less with shock absorption and allow less movement between the vertabrae. It is when we move our spine that the actual mechanical forces (caused by pressure changes to the discs from the vertabrae above and below) cause the exchange of nutrients and waste products through the process called *osmosis.*

It is healthy for your spine to move often, but what happens when you sit down in a chair and relax? First of all, sitting puts 30% more pressure on discs than standing (Oliver and Middleditch, 1991), and if you relax, you usually lean against the back of the chair plus you don't move around. With time, gravity often pulls you into a slouching position. All this leads to cutting off circulation to the discs. However, unlike skin and muscles that have nerves which immediately tell the brain there is a lack of circulation, discs, like other cartilage, do not because they do not have any nerves inside them. The nerves in the spine lie on the outside of the discs as they exit the vertabrae. The brain doesn't "feel" pain from the disc directly.

When the tissue in the disc starts deteriorating, it either becomes smaller, allowing the bones to start rubbing on one another causing degenerative arthritis, or the disc wall weakens and starts bulging out, pressing on a nerve causing pain. This process can take years, or happen quickly due to an injury.

Keeping the discs in the spine healthy is not only important for spinal flexibility and pain-free movement, but also for having good balance reactions while performing daily activities and sports throughout your life.

APPENDIX D

OTHER RESOURCES

American Heart Association Heart Power Kits (available through local offices)
Reproduced with permission.
Heart Power Kit, 1996
Copyright American Heart Association.

Ball Dynamics International, Inc.
14215 Mead St.
Longmont, CO 80504
800-752-2255 or 970-535-9090
Swiss Balls, *FitBall* video, and other educational products using Swiss Balls.

High/Scope Press
600 N. River Street
Ypsilanti, MI 48198
313-485-2000 or 800-40-PRESS
Phyllis Weikart's *Rhythmically Moving* series, videos, CDs, and books.

Kimbo Educational
Dept. T, P.O. Box 477
Long Branch, NJ 07740
800-631-2187
Musical recordings.

Silly-Cise
P.O. Box 3729
Dillon, CO 80435
800-530-3675
Scott Liebler's books and cassettes.

REFERENCES

Armstrong, T. 1994. *Multiple intelligences in the classroom*. Alexandria, VA: Association for Supervision and Curriculum Development.

Ayres, J.A. 1979. *Sensory integration and the child*. Los Angeles: Western Psychological Services.

————. 1991. *A parent's guide to understanding sensory integration*. Torrance, CA: Sensory Integration International.

Bissell, J. 1988. *Sensory motor handbook*. Torrance, CA: Sensory Integration International.

Council on Physical Education for Children (COPEC). 1994. *Developmentally appropriate practice in movement programs for young ages 3-5*: Reston, VA: National Association for Sport and Physical Education.

Fisher, Anne. 1991. *Sensory integration: Theory and practice*. Philadelphia: F.A. Davis Company.

Frick, Sheila. 1996. *Out of the mouths of babes*. Hugo, MN: PDP Press.

Gardner, H. 1993. *Multiple intelligences: The theory in practice*. New York: Basic Books.

Gatchel, Robert and Tom Mayer. 1988. *Functional restoration for spinal disorders: The sports medicine approach*. Philadelphia: Lea & Febiger.

Gray, Henry. 1966. *Anatomy of the human body*. 28th edition. Charles Mayo Goss (Ed.). Philadelphia: Lea & Febiger.

Greg and Steve. 1987. *Kids in motion*, Los Angeles: Youngheart Records.

Headly, Barbara. 1996. Testing the effectiveness of assistive devices for seating. EMG and Low Back Clinical Management. May/June 1990: 18-22.

Illi, Urs. 1994. *Balle statt stuhle im schulzimmer?* (Balls instead of chairs in the classroom.) Sporterzeihung in der schule. June 1994: 37-39.

Kempf, Hans-Dieter and Dr. Jurgan Fisher. 1993. *Rukenschule fur kinder* (Back school for children). Hamburg: Rowoholt Taschenbuch GmbH.

Klien-Vogelbach, Susanne. 1990. *Ballgymnastic zur funtionellen bewegungs lehre* (Ball Exercises for Functional Kinetics). New York: Springer Verlag.

Kucera, M. 1993. *Gymnastik mit dem hupfball* (Exercises with the therapy ball). Stuttgart: Gustav Fischer Verlag.

Liebler, Scott. 1996. Funsical fitness: A comprehensive movement and health education experience for ages 2-3/4 to 7-5/6. Byron, CA: Front Row Experiences.

Maino, D.M. 1995. *Diagnosis and management of special populations.* St. Louis: Mosby Publishing.

National Consortium for Physical Education and Recreation for Individuals With Disabilities. 1995. *Adapted physical education national standards* (APENS). Champaign, IL: Human Kinetics.

Oetter, Patricia. 1993. *M.O.R.E.: Integrating the mouth with sensory and postural functions.* Hugo, MN: PDP Press.

Oliver, Jean and Alison Middleditch. 1991. *Functional anatomy of the spine.* Oxford: Butterworth-Heinemann.

Piaget, Jean. 1977. *The origin of intelligence in the child.* New York: Penguin.

Pica, R. and R. Gardzina. 1990. *Let's move and learn.* Champaign, IL: Human Kinetics.

Pomeroy, Sandra. 1994. *Office ergonomics—Part one: The anatomy of seated work.* Philadelphia: Physical Therapy Forum.

Posner-Mayer, J. 1995. *Swiss ball applications for orthopedic and sports medicine.* Denver: Ball Dynamics International, Inc..

Posner-Mayer, J. and L. Zappala. 1994a. *The fitball workout book.* Denver, CO: Ball Dynamics International, Inc.

Ratliffe, T.and L. Ratliffe. 1994. *Teaching children fitness: Becoming a master teacher.* Champaign, IL: Human Kinetics.

Reisman, Judith. 1992. *Sensory integration inventory* (revised ed.). Hugo, MN: PDP Press.

Santrock, John W. 1996. *Child development.* Dubuque, IA: Brown & Benchmark Publishers.

Saunders, Duane H. 1995. *Evaluation, treatment and prevention of musculoskeletal disorders.* 3rd edition. Chaska, MN: Educational Opportunities.

Sweet, Waldo E. 1987. *Sport and recreation in ancient Greece: A sourcebook with translations.* New York: Oxford University Press.

Trott, M.C. 1993. *Senseabilities. Understanding sensory integration.* Tucson, AZ: Therapy Skill Builders.

Weikart, Phyllis S. 1987a. *Round the circle.* Ypsilanti, MI: High Scope Press.

Weikart, Phyllis S. 1987b. *Movement plus music.* Ypsilanti, MI: High Scope Press.

Weikart, Phyllis S. and Elizabeth B. Carlton. 1995. *Foundations in elementary education movement.* Ypsilanti, MI: High Scope Press.

Wilbarger, P. and S.L. Wilbarger. 1991. *Sensory defensiveness in children: An interventio guide for parents and other caretakers.* Santa Barbara, CA: Avant Educational Programs.

Wilder, Brigitte. 1991. *Sitz als belastung: Wir sitzen zuviel (Sitting as weightbearing: We sit too much).* Zumikon, Switzerland: Verlag SVSS.

Williams, Mary Sue and Sherry Shellenburger. 1996. *How does your engine run?* Albuquerque, NM: Therapy Works.

Young, Susan. 1988. *Movement is fun: A preschool movement program.* Torrance, CA: Sensory Integration International.

ABOUT THE AUTHORS

Anne R. Spalding *(seated)* is a recognized expert on integrating Swiss Balls into classroom settings. A physical education teacher in Boulder, Colorado, she has extensive training in developmentally appropriate practices and makes presentations on the use of Swiss Balls. Ms. Spalding is the coauthor of *Physical Education Lesson Plans: Second to Fourth Grade Program, Basic Biomechanical Principles and Fundamental Movement Skills* (1987). She also has done work in the area of integrating classroom academics into the gymnasium. Her adaptive teaching experience includes the areas of MPH, REACH, Non-Categorical, EBD, and LD students. She is a member of the American Alliance of Health, Physical Education, Recreation and Dance (AAHPERD) and the Colorado Association of Health, Physical Education, Recreation and Dance (CAHPERD). Ms. Spalding was a 1997 recipient of the "Torch Award" from the American Heart Association.

Linda Kelly *(standing, center)* has taught physical education in the Boulder Valley Public Schools since 1972. She has used Swiss Balls extensively in her teaching since 1991. Ms. Kelly has presented numerous workshops on the use of Swiss Balls. She is the recipient of teaching awards from numerous organizations, including the Foundation for Boulder Valley Schools, the Public Service Corporation, and the Colorado Heart Association. She is a member of the AAHPERD and CAHPERD.

Janet Santopietro *(standing, right)* is an Early Childhood Physical Education Specialist in Arvada, Colorado, where she contracts with area preschools to teach physical education and movement to children ages two through kindergarten. Since 1991 she has included Swiss Balls in her program. Ms. Santopietro speaks at numerous conferences and workshops that deal with early childhood education. She is a member of CAHPERD and a frequent contributor to its *Communicator* and *Journal*, Ms. Santopietro is also a member of the National Association for the Education of Young Children (NAEYC) and the Colorado AEYC.

Joanne Posner-Mayer *(standing, left)* is recognized internationally as an expert on therapeutic Swiss Ball applications. After graduating from the University of Colorado physical therapy school, she practiced in Switzerland for seven years, working with pioneering therapists using the ball. In 1980, while working at the University Orthopedic Hospital in Copenhagen, Denmark, she began lecturing on the therapeutic uses of the Swiss Ball. Since returning to the United States in the early 1980s, Ms. Mayer has taught at the University of Colorado Physical Therapy School, practiced as a physical therapist in various orthopedic and neurological settings, and has continued to lecture extensively in her area of expertise. Ms. Mayer has produced three instructional videos on exercise techniques using the Swiss Ball and has authored two previous books on Swiss Ball exercises.

Related Resources

The Brockport Physical Fitness Test Kit

Joseph P. Winnick, EdD and Francis X. Short, PED
1999 • CD-ROM for Windows • 3.5" disk for Windows

The test kit contains the three items below and the test manual, plus curl-up strips, skinfold calipers, and the PACER audiocassette and CD. The kit provides users with what they need to accurately assess fitness levels and to help students improve their fitness levels.

Fitness Challenge

Joseph P. Winnick, EdD and Francis X. Short, PED
1999 • 3.5" diskettes

The companion software that makes using the Brockport test much easier.

The Brockport Physical Fitness Test Administration Video

(Approx 30-minute videotape)
Joseph P. Winnick, EdD and Francis X. Short, PED
1999 • VHS

Demonstrates clearly how to use the Brockport Physical Fitness Test for youths with physical and mental disabilities.

The Brockport Physical Fitness Training Guide

Joseph P. Winnick, EdD and Francis X. Short, PED
1999 • Paperback • Approx 200 pp

Designed to help teachers create programs for students who need to improve in one or more areas of fitness as identified by the test.

To request more information or to order, U.S. customers call 1-800-747-4457, e-mail us at humank@hkusa.com, or visit our Web site at http://www.humankinetics.com/. Persons outside the U.S. can contact us via our Web site or use the appropriate telephone number, postal address, or e-mail address shown in the front of this book.

The American Fitness Alliance

The Brockport Physical Fitness Test and Fitness Challenge software are offered through The American Fitness Alliance (AFA), a collaborative effort of AAHPERD, the Cooper Institute for Aerobics Research (CIAR), and Human Kinetics. AFA offers additional assessment resources, which can be combined with those listed above to create a complete health-related physical education program:

- The *FITNESSGRAM* test for evaluating students' physical fitness, developed by CIAR
- The *Physical Best Program*, which identifies the components of successful health-related physical education and provides the material needed to implement it in classes
- *FitSmart*, the first national test designed to assess high school students' knowledge of concepts and principles of physical fitness